A~Z
OF
Embroidery
Stitches 2

EDITOR Susan O'Connor | ASSISTANT EDITOR Lizzie Kulinski | DESIGN AND LAYOUT Lynton Grandison

PHOTOGRAPHY Andrew Dunbar Photography | PUBLISHER Margie Bauer

DISTRIBUTION ENQUIRIES Country Bumpkin Publications, 315 Unley Road, Malvern South Australia 5061 Australia

Phone: +61 8 8372 7600 Fax: +61 8 8372 7601 Email: marketing@countrybumpkin.com.au Website: www.countrybumpkin.com.au

Published in Australia | Printed and bound in China

A - Z of Embroidery Stitches 2
ISBN 978 09775476 6 1
Copyright ©2007 Country Bumpkin Publications

CONTENTS

Threads

The origins of the first embroidery threads are unknown but it is not unreasonable to assume that the first examples of embroidery resulted from man discovering that the same stitches that were used to hold hides and cloth together for clothing, could be used to create decorative patterns.

We have come a long way from the days of crude bone needles and coarse threads, and the glorious array of embroidery threads that are now available can be quite overwhelming. While it is easy to become seduced by glowing colours and sparkling surfaces, it is always an advantage to have some understanding of the materials that you are using – those characteristics that make each thread type unique and some more suited to particular tasks than others. This will help you to avoid inappropriate choices and relieve the frustration of trying to stitch with an unsuitable thread.

So what are the characteristics that make threads different from one another?

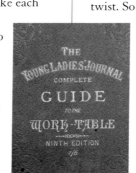

Thread Twist – 'S' twist or 'Z' twist?

Most embroidery threads are created by spinning short fibres together then combining several fine threads, or plies, to create a strong, durable thread. Exceptions to this are threads like silk filament and most metallic threads.

Fig 1

Fig 2

Fig 3

As a general rule, the longer the fibres, the stronger the thread – this is why long staple cottons and wools produce superior results to short staple ones.

The plies are twisted together in a clockwise or counter clockwise direction, resulting in a thread with either an 'S' or 'Z' twist. So how can you tell the difference? Take a single strand of thread and look carefully at the way the plies are held together. If the line of the twist goes from upper left to lower right it is an 'S' twist, like the centre of an S (fig 1).

If it goes from upper right to lower left it is a 'Z' twist, like the centre of a Z (fig 2).

Regardless of which way you hold the thread, the twist will be the same. Divisible threads will have each strand created by twisting in one direction then the bundle of strands will be held together by twisting in the opposite direction. For example, each strand of stranded cotton is created with an 'S' twist but the group of six threads are held together in a 'Z' twist (fig 3).

The majority of threads - cotton, silk, linen and wool - are 'S' twist but rayon and some silk threads tend to be 'Z' twist. So why is this important and how does this make a difference when you stitch?

For many stitches and techniques, the direction of the thread twist has little perceptible impact but there are some stitches where it becomes very obvious. This difference is made much more apparent when working with a single strand of thread.

Stem and Outline Stitch

Take a single 'S' twist thread (tapestry wool or cotton pearl are ideal) and work a line of stem stitch from left to right.

Take another length of thread and work a line of outline stitch from left to right.

Now compare the two rows of stitching - the outline stitch is very smooth and it is difficult to identify each stitch but the stem stitch is quite textured and each stitch is clearly obvious. This occurs because the thread untwists as you work the outline stitch but overtwists as you work the stem stitch. Now, if you were to take a 'Z' twist thread and do exactly the same thing, the stem stitch line would be smooth and the outline would be textured.

Bullion Knots

Take a single 'S' twist thread and work a bullion knot, wrapping the thread in a clockwise direction around the needle.

Work a second knot, this time wrapping the thread in a counter clockwise direction.

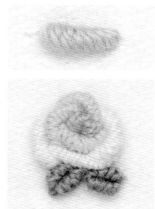

'S' twist thread wrapped clockwise

'S' twist thread wrapped counter clockwise

The first knot will be very smooth as the thread plies have been untwisted as you wrap around the needle and they are lying next to one another. The second knot will be textured with each thread wrap quite discernible as the plies are more tightly twisted together. If you were to repeat this exercise with a 'Z' twist thread, the results would be the opposite – the knot that was wrapped clockwise around the needle will be textured, the one wrapped counter clockwise will be smooth.

High twist or low twist?

The amount of twist impacts not only on the appearance of a thread but also on its strength and performance. So how can you tell if a thread is high or low twist? Visually, a high twist thread will have more twists per centimetre than a low twist one (fig 4). As this is often difficult to see, you can usually tell by squeezing the thread between your thumb and index finger A high twist thread will not flatten easily and retains its roundness, even under pressure. A low twist thread will flatten easily and is difficult to discern between your fingers.

Fig 4

High twist threads are usually stronger and less likely to abrade when worked than low twist threads.

As you are stitching, it is important to ensure that the twist in the thread stays consistent or you will find that the surface of your work will change. As a thread untwists it will reflect more light and appear shinier. If it overtwists it will lose its sheen and appear dull. This is particularly noticeable when working satin stitch. Allow the needle to hang freely every now and then so that the thread can regain its natural twist or add twist with your fingers.

High twist threads such as cotton pearl and buttonhole twists are non-divisible, strong, round threads that retain their shape and sit up on the surface of the fabric. This makes them more suitable when good stitch definition is important, but less appropriate to techniques like thread painting where it is vital that the stitches merge together.

High twist threads are easier to use when working woven or detached techniques, eg needlewoven picots, as the thread holds together and the plies are less likely to split.

Which needle?

High twist threads can be more difficult to thread into a needle as the thread will not flatten as easily to fit through the eye. If you look closely at the eye of a needle, regardless of type, it will be elongated rather than round, so it helps to make the thread fit the eye. Whatever type of needle you choose, ensure that the eye is large enough to allow the thread to pass through effortlessly without untwisting.

Silk, wool, cotton or...

We are lucky to have a large range of fibres available, and there are some exciting new ones such as soy and bamboo coming onto the market. Fibre choice can be determined by a number of factors including appearance, performance and care requirements.

Cotton is the most widely available embroidery thread and it comes in a variety of finishes; stranded cotton, soft cotton, cotton pearl and broder spécial (also known as coton à broder) are widely available. Cotton threads are usually colourfast (be careful with some overdyed threads) and have a medium lustre, but cotton is not a strong fibre and may fluff easily if not handled correctly.

Silk is also available in a number of different types; stranded, buttonhole twist, silk pearl and filament are some of the most common threads. Silk has a wonderful sheen, is incredibly strong but not always colourfast, so check the care requirements on the label. Silk threads fall into two basic categories: spun silk threads where short lengths of fibre are spun together and filament silk threads where the continuous silk filament is wound off the cocoon. Filament silks have superior strength and superb high lustre but can be challenging to use.

Wool is a wonderful fibre to embroider with - soft, warm and incredibly forgiving. It has a fibrous, matt surface and comes in a number of weights ranging from thick tapestry wool to fine crewel yarns. Wool threads are washable, colourfast and reasonably strong. They can, however, vary in appearance and durability depending on the type of wool used. For example, Shetland wool fibre is coarse and wiry but merino is fine, soft and smooth.

No other thread evokes such a love/hate relationship as rayon. Made from cellulose, rayon threads are incomparably lustrous and very strong but they also possess a springy, 'mind of their own' quality that makes them tricky to use and, consequently, disliked by some embroiderers. Despite this, others love the brilliant sheen and the exciting way that this thread contrasts with matt and low sheen threads.

There are other fibres on the market, plus numerous blends, but no matter what you choose, always check the label for fibre content and care requirements.

If you are unsure of the colourfastness of a thread, work a few stitches onto fabric, then wash to check for colour bleed.

Some of the points covered here will seem to make a very minor difference but by increasing your understanding of the nature of the materials that you are using, you will have much better control over the final look of your embroidery - often it is small details that make the difference between something being good and being great!

Needles

Embroidery needles come in such a large range of different styles and sizes that it can be confusing. How do you know which needle you have once it is removed from the packet?

The easiest way to avoid confusion arising is to familiarise yourself with the characteristics that make each needle unique. A good starting point is the type of eye. Needles can be classified as either large or small eyed.

Large eyed needles are easily identified by the long narrow eye that makes them easier to thread. The large eye also creates a definite bulge at the end of the needle. Crewel, chenille, tapestry and darners are all large eyed needles.

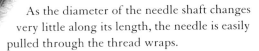

Crewel

A crewel needle (sometimes known as an embroidery needle), is probably the most familiar needle. Crewel needles have a sharp tip and are widely available in sizes 10 (fine) to 1 (thick). They are used for most embroidery and smocking as they are a good all-purpose needle.

Chenille

Chenille needles look like large crewel needles and are used for wool and silk ribbon embroidery. They also have a sharp tip and are available in sizes 26 (fine) to 14 (thick).

Tapestry

Tapestry needles are very similar to chenille needles in size, the major difference is the tip. A tapestry needle has a blunt tip making it suitable for needlepoint, canvas work, pulled and drawn thread techniques or in any situation where it is important not to split the fabric threads.

Tapestry needles are available in sizes 28 (fine) to 16 (thick).

Darners

Darners (sometimes known as yarn or wool darners), can have a blunt or sharp tip and look like large chenille or tapestry needles. Some darners also have a long shaft and are known as long darners. Knitters use them for sewing up garments and they are suitable for any thick thread.

Small eyed needles have a small round eye that makes very little difference to the shaft thickness.

Sharps, betweens, milliner's and beading needles can all be classified as small eyed.

Sharps

A sharp is a good all-purpose needle that is particularly suited to fine embroidery. Sharps are most commonly available in sizes 12 (fine), sometimes called a hand appliqué needle, to 1 (thick).

Betweens

Betweens (or quilting needles) are similar to sharps but they have a very short shaft. Quilters traditionally use betweens as they enable the stitcher to work quickly and evenly.

Milliner's

Milliner (straw) needles have a long shaft and are essential when working bullion knots with most types of threads.

As the diameter of the needle shaft changes very little along its length, the needle is easily pulled through the thread wraps.

These needles were traditionally used by milliners when making hats. They are available in sizes 11 (fine) to 1 (thick).

Beading

Beading needles have a very fine, long shaft and are not suited for general embroidery as the shaft is easily bent. They are manufactured specifically for stitching very fine beads with small holes. Many beads can be applied using a fine sharp or milliner's needle.

The needles listed are those most commonly used for embroidery. Stitch instructions will usually include a specific needle or needles for a project. It is often possible to substitute another needle that you may already have.

Needle choice is a very personal thing. Some people prefer to use a sharp, some a crewel, some a between. There are some embroidery techniques that do require a specific needle but for most tasks, choose a needle that you feel comfortable using. Regardless of the type of needle that you choose, it should be good quality with a straight, smooth shaft and clean eye. Discard any needles that are burred, bent, or damaged in any way. If the nickel plating starts to flake off the steel it should also be discarded as it will not pass through the fabric as smoothly and once exposed to the air, the steel will rust. The eye of the needle should be large enough to accommodate the thread without wearing or distorting the thread twist. If the needle eye is too small or narrow, the thread will untwist as it is pulled through. To choose the correct size of needle for the thread, the shaft of the needle should be at least the same diameter as the thread so that, as it passes through the fabric, it opens a hole large enough for the thread to follow through without becoming worn or abraded.

Needles can be purchased in single or multi-size packs. A multi-size pack of each needle type will make a good needle collection. Always keep your needles clean and dry. Discard any needles that are damaged and you will find that you will get many hours of use from these essential embroidery tools.

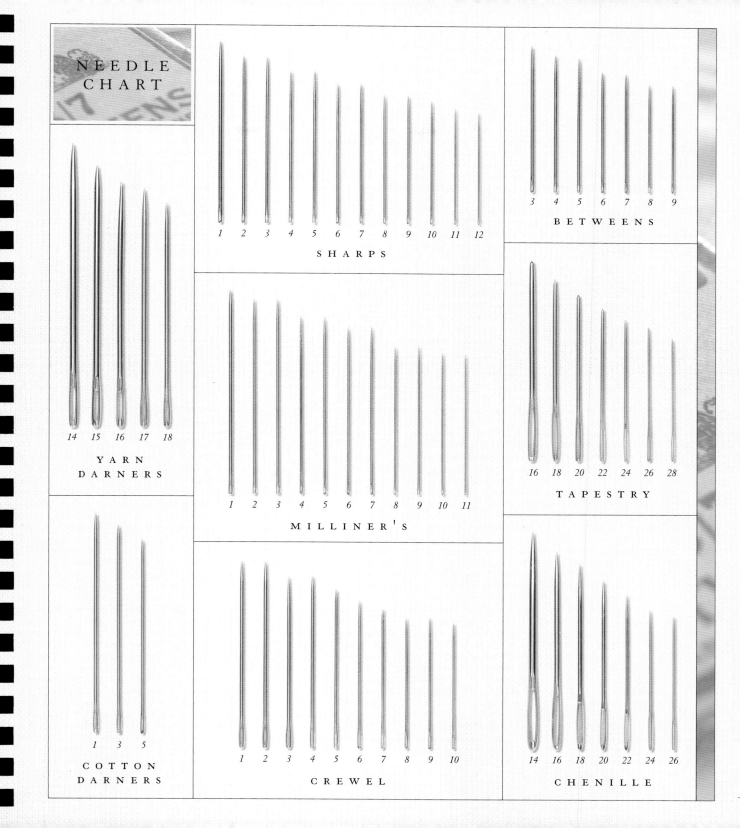

NEEDLE
CHART

YARN
DARNERS

14 15 16 17 18

COTTON
DARNERS

1 3 5

SHARPS

1 2 3 4 5 6 7 8 9 10 11 12

MILLINER'S

1 2 3 4 5 6 7 8 9 10 11

CREWEL

1 2 3 4 5 6 7 8 9 10

BETWEENS

3 4 5 6 7 8 9

TAPESTRY

16 18 20 22 24 26 28

CHENILLE

14 16 18 20 22 24 26

Hoops

An embroidery hoop, or frame, is a tensioning device. Its role is to hold the fabric firmly while the stitches are being worked, enabling the embroiderer to use the taut fabric to tension the stitches properly and avoid unsightly puckering. Embroiderers who do not use a hoop usually do this in some other way such as wrapping the fabric tightly over their fingers.

Embroidery worked in a hoop is done using the 'stab' method - each stitch is made using two movements; the needle is taken to the back of the fabric, pulled through, and then returned to the front. Stitches that are 'sewn' are worked in one movement; the needle goes to the back of the fabric then returns to the front in one action. This technique is also known as 'skimming' or 'scooping' and for stitches like chain, stem, back and running stitch, is a fast and effective way of working. Stitches that are 'sewn' should not be worked in a hoop as the surface tension of the fabric will be compromised to enable the needle to pass in and out easliy.

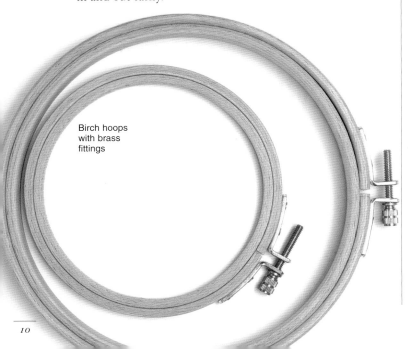

Birch hoops
with brass
fittings

Choosing and preparing a hoop

Hoops are available in wood and plastic and the quality of both is quite variable. What you choose to buy is often influenced by what is available but it is well worth pursuing the very best of what is manufactured. Good quality, white birch hoops with brass fittings are manufactured in Germany and are superior to anything else on the market. The rings are made from laminated timber that is well finished and does not splinter. The fittings are brass and much stronger than the cheaper white metal that is found on inferior hoops. The brass does not bend when the hoop is tightened and enables the hoop to maintain a high level of tension.

Most importantly, the tightening screw has a slot in the end that allows the hoop to be tightened with a screw driver so that a drum tight surface can be achieved and maintained. A chunky handled screwdriver is much easier to use than a thin handled one and is a handy addition to your sewing kit.

It is advisable to bind the inner ring of the hoop as this will protect the fabric and stop it from sliding against the wood. Comm-ercial bias binding is ideal as it is a ready made, thin bias strip. You may prefer it over twill tape as it is not as thick and does not leave ridges when it is wrapped. Choose a light colour that will not shed coloured fibre onto the fabric – white is best. Iron

the bias flat then wrap it around the inner ring, only just overlapping the edges. Stitch the ends together to secure.

Round hoops come in three depths 7mm (5/16"), 16mm (5/8") and 25mm (1") and sizes vary from 10cm (4") up to 30cm (12").

Specialty hoops

Most hoops are round but there are also rectangles and squares with rounded corners that are a much more practical shape for most projects. These hoops fit together one way and are stamped on both rings to indicate this. They usually do not require binding as they fit together so well. Some of these hoops have a variation of the tensioning screw that pulls the outer hoop together without pushing it down, as the conventional one does. This is a vastly superior fitting and these hoops are priced accordingly but are well worth it.

Having the hoop supported in some way will make stitching a much more pleasurable task. A seat hoop or frame is the perfect solution and a worthwhile investment. This has a flat wooden base with an adjustable vertical stem that holds the hoop at the top supported on an adjustable upright. You simply sit on the base and you don't need to hold the hoop at all. This allows you to stitch with two hands, your favoured hand beneath the work, and can halve your stitching time. Various hoops sizes are available.

Getting the most out of a hoop

Like most tools, you get the most out of a hoop if you use it properly. There is really no value in having your fabric in a hoop if you allow it to become slack and are maintaining the tension with a finger beneath the work!

Take the time to put the fabric in the hoop carefully; tightening both the hoop and the fabric gradually until you have a firm, even surface. Ensure that the weave of the fabric remains true as any distortions will become painfully obvious when the hoop is removed. Only pull the straight grain of the fabric, not the bias as it will stretch and distort the grain. Once the fabric is taut, use the screwdriver to tighten the screw as much as you can. This will ensure that the fabric is held firmly and, as long as you don't put your fingers on the fabric, it will stay that way.

Check the surface of the fabric regularly while you are working and if you notice it becoming slack, tighten it again.

Hold the hoop by the outer ring without touching the fabric. If you work at a table you can sit the hoop on the edge and hold it in place with a heavy book. This way you can work hands free.

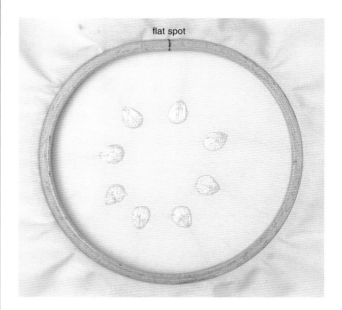

When using a hoop for the first time, mark the point of the inner ring that sits directly beneath the tensioning screw. When using the hoop again, always position this back in the same place as you will find that the inner ring becomes slightly flattened at this point and it is impossible to get a good fit unless this flat spot is in the right place.

Keeping it clean

There is nothing more disheartening than finishing a piece of embroidery and removing the hoop to find that you have a dirty ring around your fabric. No matter how often you wash your hands, skin secretes natural oils that attract dirt and this is all easily transferred to the fabric, particularly around the edge of the hoop.

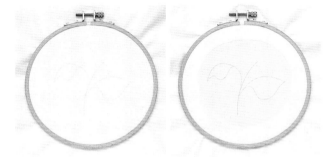

To avoid this problem you can:

> Place a piece of thin fabric, voile or muslin, over your fabric when you place it in the hoop. Tighten both fabrics separately then carefully cut away the top layer to expose the part of the design that you are working on (shown right).

> Do the same thing with a piece of cling film.

> Tack tissue paper over the surface of the fabric then cut away the area that you are working on.

> When each area of stitching is complete, tack a piece of fabric or tissue paper over it to protect the finished work.

> Stretch a shower cap over the hoop. The elasticised edge will hold it in place and you can cut away the plastic over the area that you are working.

Binding a hoop

To protect the fabric from the wood and to prevent the fabric from slipping, it is advisable to bind the inner hoop with tape or bias binding. To mount the fabric, stretch the section of the fabric to be worked over the inner ring. Keep the grain of the fabric square, press down the outer

ring and tighten the screw. Good quality hoops with screws that can be tightened with a screwdriver give the best results.

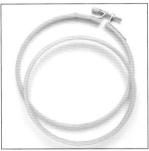

1. Separate the two pieces of the hoop.

2. Using bias binding ironed flat, hold the end and wrap around the inner ring of the hoop.

3. Work small back stitches at the edge of the bias binding.

4. Wrap the hoop with the binding ensuring there are no creases.

5. When reaching the starting point, cut off the excess binding and work small back stitches to secure.

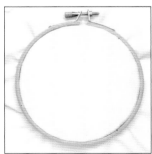

6. Mount the fabric in the hoop.

Scissors

The most important tool for any embroiderer is a pair of good quality embroidery scissors. There are many different brands and styles to choose from and it pays, in the long run, to buy the very best pair that you can. The following companies make beautiful, premium quality scissors – Dovo, Wasa and Gingher. Kai is another excellent brand but with a more functional look. These scissors can be expensive but they are certainly worth it as they will give you many years of use. Put a pair at the top of your gift wish list! Take good care of them and ensure that they are only used for cutting threads and fabric. A weighted scissor fob will ensure that, if dropped, they will land handles first, avoiding damaging the tips. Have them professionally sharpened if they begin to develop a dull spot.

Stitch tension

Even stitch tension is an important element in obtaining an excellent finish to your embroidery.

An embroidery hoop or frame will help but only if you keep the fabric consistently taut whilst you are working. Once the fabric is tight you can use the fabric tension to tension each stitch, pulling the thread until it is firm against the fabric surface. In this way you are guaranteed an even tension.

Adjust and tighten the hoop or frame when necessary. If you are working 'in the hand', wrap the fabric over the fingers of your other hand (the one that you are not using to stitch). Again, this will put tension on the fabric and allow you to tighten the stitches against the fabric. Washing and pressing also improves the embroidery surface and can help even out your stitches.

ALTERNATING DIAGONAL STITCH

This stitch is worked using two different threads and can be used to create borders and stems. Mark a guideline onto the fabric.

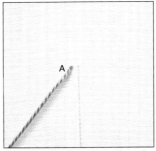

1. Bring the first thread to the front at A, to the left of the beginning of the marked line.

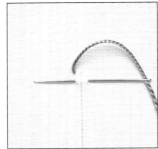

2. Take the needle from right to left across the line a short distance below. The needle is at right angles to the line.

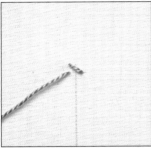

3. Pull the thread through to form the first diagonal stitch.

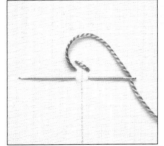

4. Take the needle from right to left across the line a short distance below. Ensure that the stitches are parallel.

5. Pull the thread through. Continue working to the end of the line. Take the needle to the back and secure.

6. Change thread. Bring the thread to the front at B.

7. Work a diagonal straight stitch between the first and second stitches.

8. Pull the thread through. Work a diagonal straight stitch between the second and third stitches.

9. Continue working in the same manner to the end. Take the needle to the back and secure.

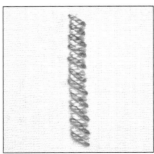

10. Completed alternating diagonal stitch.

ANTWERP EDGING STITCH

Also known as knot stitch and knotted blanket stitch, this is a decorative edging used on a hemmed edge.

Most thread types are suitable but round, high twist threads such as cotton perlé are the most effective. Multiple rows can be worked, stitching through the loops of the previous rows to create an open lacy edge. Work from left to right.

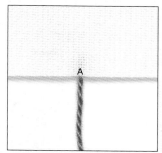

1. Anchor the thread and emerge through the hem edge at A.

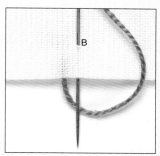

2. Take the needle through the fabric at B. Ensure the thread is under the tip of the needle.

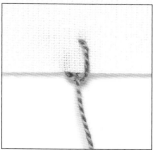

3. Pull the thread through.

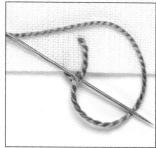

4. Take the needle behind the two threads. Ensure the working thread is under the tip of the needle.

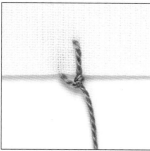

5. Pull the thread through and tighten to form a knot.

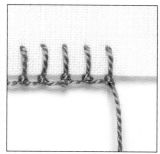

6. Continue working in this manner along the hem edge.

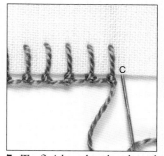

7. To finish, take the thread through the hem edge at C.

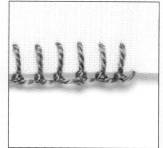

8. Secure the thread. Completed Antwerp edging stitch.

ARMENIAN EDGING STITCH

This pretty stitch creates a narrow scalloped edge. It can be stitched as a single row or multiple rows can be worked to create a lacy edge. The stitch is worked from left to right.

1. Bring the thread to the front of the seam line at A.

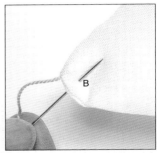

2. Take a small stitch through the seam, emerging at B.

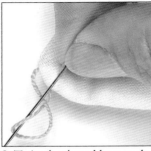

3. Twist the thread loop to the right, forming a figure eight. Take the needle under and through the lower loop.

4. Pull the stitch firmly to form a knot. Completed first stitch.

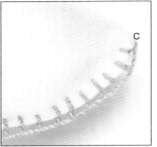

5. Repeat steps 2 - 4 at small intervals to the end of the row. Take the needle through the seam at C a short distance from the last knot and secure.

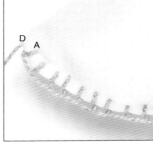

6. Detached Armenian edging stitch. Bring the thread to the front at D, to the left of A.

7. Slide the needle under the loop of the first stitch in the first row.

8. Repeat step 3.

9. Pull the thread firmly, forming a knot around the loop of the first stitch.

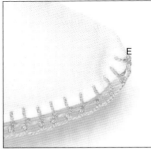

10. Continue to work the knots into the loops of the first row. End off at E a short distance from the last knot.

BACK STITCH — INTERLACED

Interlaced back stitch is worked on a foundation of back stitch. When working the interlacing, the needle does not pierce the fabric except at the beginning and end. Use a tapestry needle to work the interlacing to prevent the needle catching the fabric or thread.

1. Work a foundation row of back stitches.

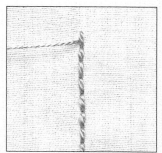

2. Using a new thread, bring it to the front halfway along the first back stitch.

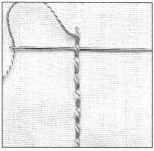

3. Slide the needle from left to right under the second back stitch.

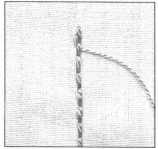

4. Pull the thread through until it rests gently against the back stitches.

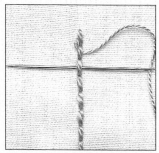

5. Slide the needle from right to left under the third back stitch.

6. Pull the thread through until it rests gently against the back stitches. Continue working stitches to the end in the same manner.

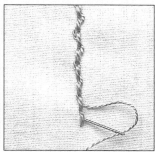

7. Take the needle to the back of the fabric halfway along the last back stitch and secure.

8. Using a new thread, bring the thread to the front halfway along the first back stitch.

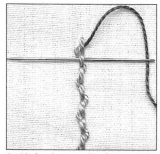

9. Slide the needle from right to left under the second back stitch and the first interlacing thread.

10. Continue working stitches as a mirror image of the first half. End off the thread in the same manner as before.

BACK STITCH — SPIDER WEB

This stitch is also known as ribbed spider web. Here eight spokes are worked to form the framework for the back stitching but any number of spokes may be used. To ensure you do not split the threads or snag the fabric, take the needle under the spokes, eye first, or use a tapestry needle.

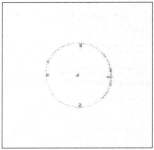

1. Draw a circle and mark the centre with a dot. Mark the outer edge of the circle into quarters.

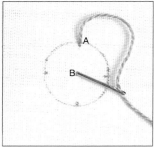

2. Bring the thread to the front at A. Take it to the back at B.

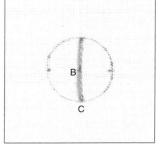

3. Pull the thread through. Emerge at C. Take the needle to the back B.

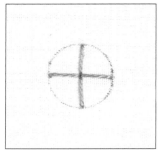

4. Work two more stitches in the same manner.

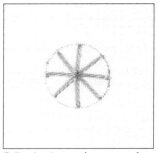

5. Beginning at the outer edge, work a straight stitch between the quarter marks. You will have eight straight stitches.

6. Bring the thread to the front to the left of one spoke and as close as possible to B.

7. Take the needle back over the spoke. Slide under this spoke and the next spoke to the left.

8. Tighten the thread until it wraps snugly around the first spoke but does not distort it.

9. Take the needle back over the second spoke. Slide it under the second and third spokes.

10. Tighten the thread to complete the second stitch.

11. Continue working stitches in the same manner, spiralling them around the spokes and keeping the rows close together.

12. After the last stitch, take the needle to the back on the right hand side of the last used spoke.

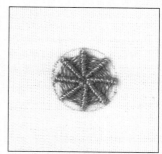

13. Pull the thread through and secure on the back.

BACK STITCH — ZIGZAG

This effective stitch is quick and easy to work. When stitched in mirror-image rows it forms a diamond pattern.

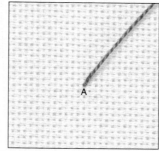

1. Bring the thread to the front at A.

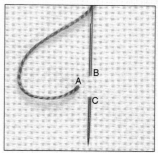

2. Insert the needle at B, two threads above and two to the right of A. Emerge at C, four threads below B.

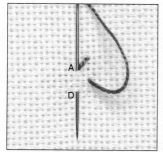

3. Pull the thread through. Insert the needle at A and emerge at D, four threads below A.

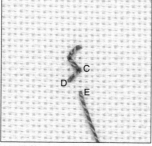

4. Pull the thread through. Work a stitch from D to C, emerging at E, four threads below C.

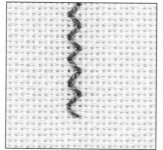

5. Continue in this manner to the end of the row.

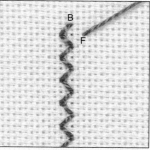

6. Bring the thread to the front at F, two threads to the left and two threads below B.

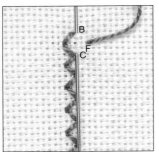

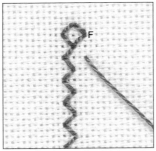

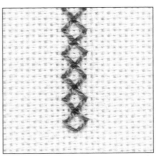

7. Insert the needle at B and emerge at C, working through the same holes in the fabric.

8. Pull through. Take the thread to the back at F and emerge four threads below. Pull through.

9. Continue in this manner, working into the holes of the previous row.

BASKET STITCH

Also known as Spanish stitch and plait stitch, this stitch produces a lovely braided line and can be worked so that the stitches are open, giving a lacy effect, or closed to create a solid line of colour. It is suited to most thread types. Mark parallel lines onto the fabric.

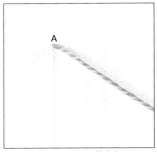

1. Mark two parallel lines on the fabric. Bring the needle to the front at the top of the left-hand line at A.

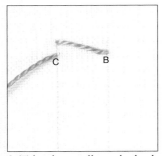

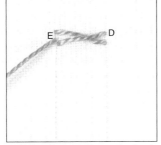

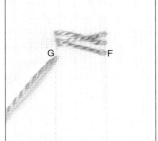

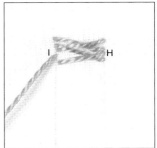

2. Take the needle to the back at B and emerge at C, directly opposite.

3. Take the needle to the back above the first stitch at D. Emerge just below the first stitch at E.

4. Take the needle to the back at F and emerge at G, directly opposite.

5. Take the needle to the back above the third stitch at H. Emerge below the third stitch at I.

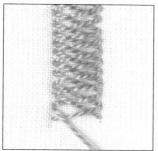
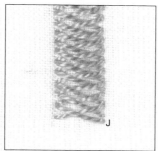

6. Continue working in this manner to the end of the shape.

7. Take the thread to the back at J and secure. Open basket stitch.

8. Closed basket stitch.

BASQUE STITCH

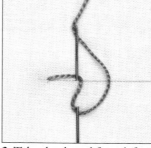
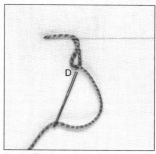

1. Bring the thread to the front at A. Take a stitch from B to C, keeping the thread above the needle.

2. Take the thread from left to right behind the eye end and under the tip of the needle. Pull the thread firmly.

3. Pull the thread through. Take the needle to the back at D, anchoring the thread loop.

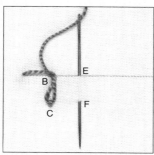
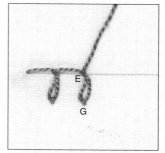
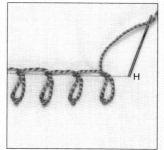

4. Bring the needle to the front at B, through the same hole in the fabric.

5. Take a second stitch from E to F, ensuring the distance is the same as B to C.

6. Complete the second stitch following steps 2 and 3, anchoring the chain at G and re-emerging at E.

7. Continue in this manner to the end of the row. To end off, take the thread to the back at H and secure.

BEAD EDGING — SINGLE

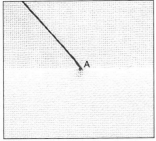

1. Bring the thread to the front at A and work a small securing stitch.

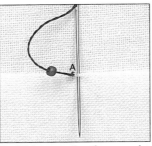

2. Slide one bead onto the needle. Insert the needle one bead length from A. Emerge 1mm ($^1/_{16}$") in from the edge.

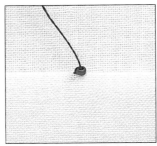

3. Pull the thread through. Insert the needle through the bead. Standing the bead on its side, pull through firmly.

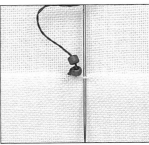

4. Thread a bead onto the needle. Insert the needle one bead length from the first bead. Emerge 1mm ($^1/_{16}$") down from the edge.

5. Pull thread through. Insert the needle through the bead and pull through firmly. The second bead touches the first.

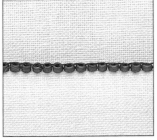

6. Continue in the same manner. Finish the last bead and secure on the back.

BEADED HEDEBO EDGE

A Hedebo edge forms a decorative scalloped finish. A foundation of large and small cross stitches is embroidered first at the marked positions and Hedebo stitch and beading are worked over this to form the scallops.

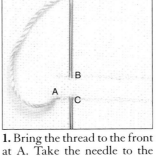

1. Bring the thread to the front at A. Take the needle to the back at B and emerge at C.

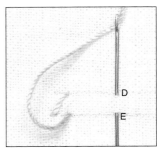

2. Pull the thread through. Take the needle from D to E.

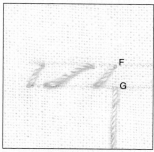

3. Pull the thread through. Take the needle from F to G. Pull the thread through.

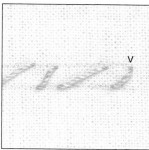

4. Continue, repeating steps 1 - 3. Take the thread to the back at V.

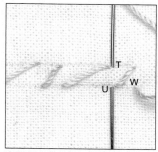

5. Bring the thread to the front at W. Take the needle from T to U through previously used holes in the fabric.

6. Pull the thread through. Continue working the remaining half of the cross stitches, finishing above A.

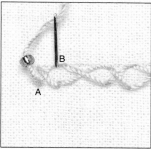

7. Bring the needle to the front at A, pick up a seed bead and take the needle to the back at B.

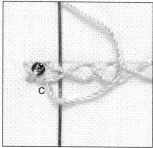

8. Pull the thread through and emerge at C. Slide the needle under the cross stitches keeping the thread over the needle.

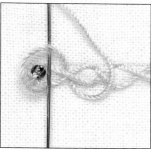

9. Pull the thread through, until a small loop is formed. Take the needle through the loop as shown.

10. Pull the thread until the stitch sits snugly.

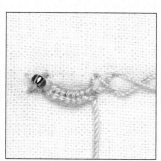

11. Repeat steps 8 - 10, packing the stitches closely so that a scallop is formed.

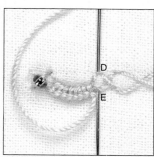

12. Take the needle to the back at D and emerge at E.

13. Pull the thread through and repeat steps 7 - 12 to complete the remaining scallops.

BLANKET STITCH – ALTERNATING

A lovely spiked line stitch, alternating blanket stitch is ideal for use as a border or to create fine stems. Mark a line onto the fabric.

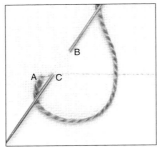

1. Bring the thread to the front at A. Take the needle to the back at B and emerge at C, ensuring that the thread is under the tip of the needle.

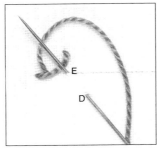

2. Take the needle to the back at D and emerge at E, ensuring that the thread is under the tip of the needle.

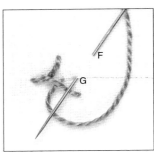

3. Take the needle from F to G, ensuring that the thread is under the tip of the needle.

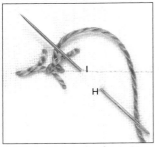

4. Take the needle from H to I, ensuring that the thread is under the tip of the needle.

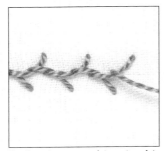

5. Continue working in this manner to the end of the row.

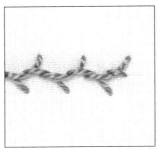

6. Take the needle to the back and secure.

BLANKET STITCH – EYELET

Blanket stitch eyelets can be used in counted thread work or surface embroidery. The stitches are pulled firmly to create a hole in the centre.
The arrow indicates the top of the fabric.

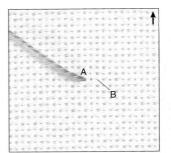

1. Bring the thread to the front at A, two fabric threads to the left of the centre of the eyelet, B.

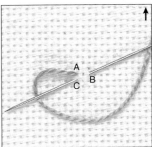

2. Insert the needle at B. Emerge at C, one thread below A. Keep the thread under the needle.

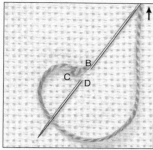

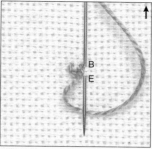

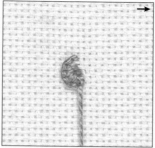

3. Pull through firmly. Insert the needle at B and emerge at D, one thread below and one to the right of C, keeping the thread under the needle.

4. Pull through firmly. Insert the needle at B and emerge at E, two threads below B.

5. Pull through. Turn the fabric. Repeat steps 2 to 4, pulling each stitch firmly to form a hole at the centre.

6. Repeat step 5 for the third quarter of the eyelet.

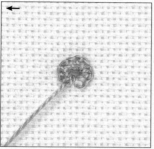

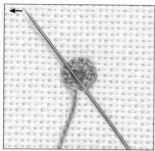

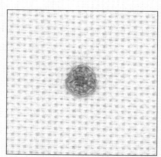

7. Turn the fabric. Repeat steps 2 and 3. Pull through firmly.

8. Slide the needle under the purl edge of the first stitch.

9. Take the thread to the back through the centre and secure.

BLANKET STITCH — EYELET FLOWER

Bullion loops are worked around an eyelet to create petals. Use a milliner's needle for the bullion loop petals.

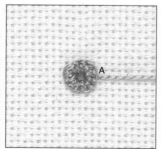

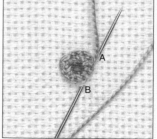

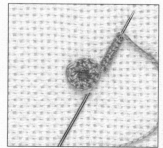

1. Bring the thread to the front at A, just outside the purl edge of the eyelet.

2. Insert the needle a short distance away from where it emerged (B). Re-emerge at A.

3. Wrap the thread the required number of times around the needle.

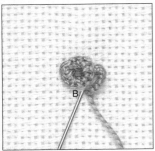 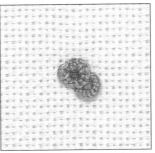 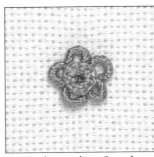 

4. Pull the needle and thread through the wraps. Take the needle to the back at B.

5. Tighten the wraps into a loop.

6. Work another four loops evenly around the edge of the eyelet in the same manner.

BLANKET STITCH — GERMAN KNOTTED

This decorative variation of blanket stitch is formed by working blanket stitches on a slight angle and looping each pair of stitches together.

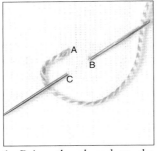 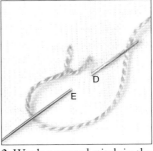 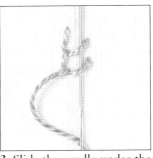

1. Bring the thread to the front at A. Take the needle to the back at B and emerge at C, keeping the thread under the needle.

2. Work a second stitch in the same manner from D to E.

3. Slide the needle under the two parallel stitches without picking up any fabric.

 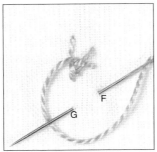  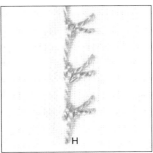

4. Pull the thread through and loop it to the left.

5. Work the next stitch from F to G. Ensure that the thread is under the tip of the needle.

6. Continue working in this manner to the end of the row, spacing the stitches in pairs.

7. Take the thread to the back at H and secure.

BLANKET STITCH — UP AND DOWN

In this variation of blanket stitch, the stitches are worked back-to-back, creating double upright stitches.

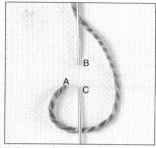

1. Bring thread to the front at A. Take needle to the back at B and emerge at C, keeping the thread under the needle.

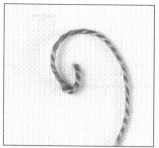

2. Hold the first stitch in place and loop the thread as shown.

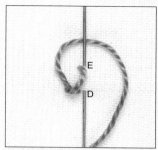

3. Work a stitch from D to E.

4. Pull the thread through in a downward motion, forming a loop around the stitches.

5. Work a second pair of taller stitches in the same manner, to the right of the first pair.

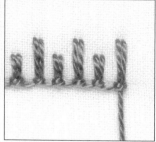

6. Continue to work evenly spaced stitches in this manner, alternating the length of each pair of stitches.

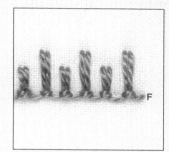

7. To end off, take the needle to the back at F.

BLANKET STITCH — LEAF

Blanket stitch is ideal for working leaf shapes as it creates an attractive beaded edge.

1. First half of leaf. Bring the thread to the front at A, at the base of the leaf shape.

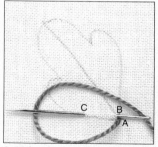

2. Take the needle to the back at B. Emerge at C. Ensure the thread is under the tip of the needle.

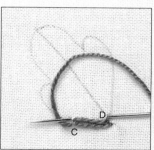

3. Pull the thread through. Take the needle to back at D. Emerge on the outer edge just above C.

blanket stitch - leaf | *continued*

4. Pull thread through. Continue, inserting the needle on the centre vein marking. Keep stitches angled and close together following leaf shape.

5. When reaching the tip, take the needle to the back over the last stitch.

6. Secure the thread on the back. Completed first half of leaf.

7. Starting at base work in the same manner as the first half. Completed second half of leaf.

BLANKET STITCH — KNOTTED

In this variation of blanket stitch, a knot is worked at the tip of each vertical stitch. Some practice is required to keep the knots even and the same size.

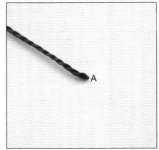

1. Bring the thread to the front at A.

2. Wrap the thread once around your left thumb as shown.

3. Slide the needle from bottom to top under the loop.

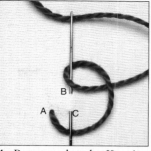

4. Remove thumb. Keeping the loop on the needle, take the needle from B to C. Ensure the thread is under the tip of the needle.

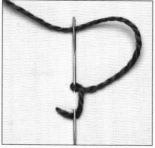

5. Pull the thread firmly so the emerging thread is taut and the loop tightens around the needle.

6. Keeping your left thumb over the loop (thumb not shown), pull the thread through.

7. Completed first stitch.

8. Wrap the thread around your left thumb as shown.

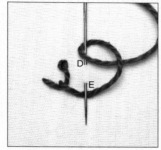

9. Slide the needle from bottom to top through the loop. Keeping the loop on the needle, take the needle to the back at D and emerge at E.

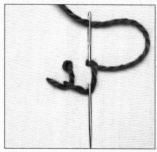

10. Tighten the thread, ensuring the thread is under the tip of the needle.

11. Pull the thread through. Completed second stitch.

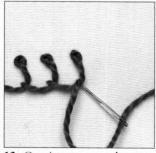

12. Continue across the row. To anchor the last stitch, take the needle over the adjacent thread and to the back.

13. Pull the thread through and secure.

BLANKET STITCH — OPEN DETACHED

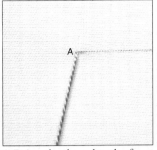

1. Bring the thread to the front at A, on the left hand side.

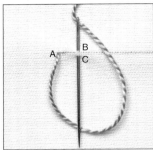

2. Take needle from B to C, a short distance away to the right. Ensure the thread lies under the needle.

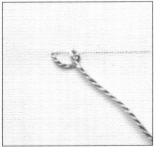

3. Gently pull the thread through until a tiny loop is formed. Do not pull the stitch tight.

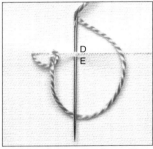

4. Take the needle from D to E, a short distance away to the right. Ensure the thread is under the needle.

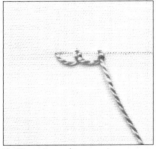

5. Keeping the tension even, pull the thread through as before to form the second stitch.

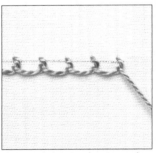

6. Continue working stitches in the same manner to the end of the row.

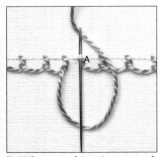

7. When working in a round, work the last stitch so the needle re-emerges at A.

8. Take the needle to the back, over the loop. Emerge directly below the first horizontal thread, ready to begin row 2.

9. Pull the thread through.

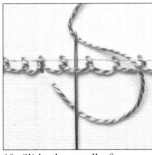

10. Slide the needle from top to bottom under the second horizontal thread in the first row. Ensure the thread is under the needle.

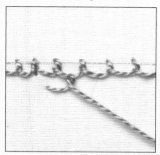

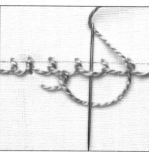

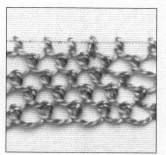

11. Gently pull the thread through until it rests against the horizontal thread.

12. Slide the needle under the next horizontal thread in the same manner as before. Gently pull the thread through.

13. Continue working stitches to the end of the row in the same manner. End off as before.

14. Continue working the required number of rows.

BLANKET STITCH — PADDED BUTTONHOLE

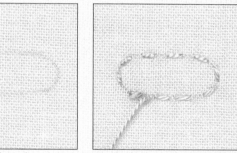

1. Secure the thread with tiny running stitches and a split back stitch.

2. Work a row of running stitch along the marked line.

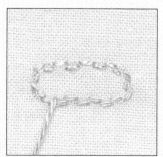

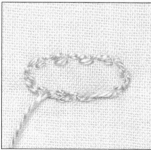

3. Work a second row of running stitch just inside the first, staggering the stitches.

4. Add a second layer of running stitches on top, splitting the stitches of the first row.

5. Repeat over the second row of running stitch. Secure the thread with split back stitch over the padding.

6. Using very sharp pointed scissors, trim the fabric away inside the stitches.

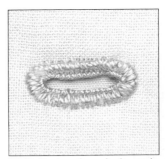

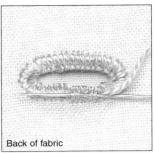

Back of fabric

7. Bring the thread to the front through the hole.

8. Take the needle through the fabric on the outside of the stitches. Bring through the hole, keeping the thread under the tip of the needle.

9. Pull the thread through. Continue to work blanket stitch very closely over the padding in the same manner. Take the thread to the back.

10. Complete the last stitch, by taking the needle through the purl of the first stitch. Secure the thread under the blanket stitches.

BLANKET STITCH — SCALLOP EDGING

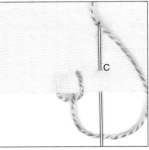

1. Bring the thread to the front at A. Take the needle to the back at B. Ensure the thread is under the tip of the needle.

2. Pull the thread through until the stitch sits loosely against the folded edge of the fabric.

3. Take the needle to the back at C. Ensure the thread is under the tip of the needle.

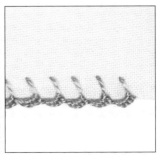

4. Repeat step 2. Slide the needle through the stitch as shown, keeping the thread under the tip of the needle.

5. Pull the thread through until the stitch sits snugly against the previous thread, forming a detached blanket stitch.

6. Work three detached stitches over the same thread close to the first. Completed first scallop.

7. Repeat steps 3 - 6 for the required distance. To end off, take needle to the back over the last loop and secure.

BLANKET STITCH — SPACED FILLING

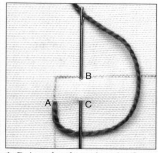

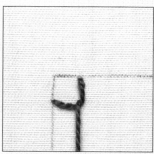

1. Bring the thread to the front at A. Take the needle from B to C, ensuring the thread lies under the tip of the needle.

2. Pull the thread through until the loop rests gently against the emerging thread.

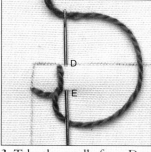

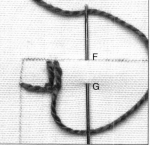

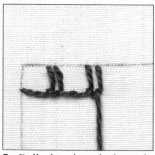

3. Take the needle from D to E. The second stitch is the same height as the previous stitch and very close to it.

4. Pull the thread through as before. Take the needle from F to G. This stitch is the same height as the previous stitches but a short distance away.

5. Pull the thread through. Work a fourth stitch very close to the third stitch.

6. Continue working pairs of stitches across the row in the same manner.

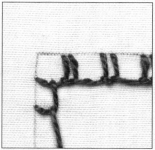

7. Take the thread to the back at the side of the shape. Secure the thread on the back.

8. Bring the thread to the front at H.

9. Take needle to back at I and emerge at J.

10. Pull the thread through ensuring the thread is under the tip of the needle.

blanket stitch - spaced filling | *continued*

11. Work a second stitch in the same manner, very close to the first stitch.

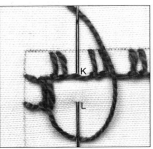

12. Take the needle to the back at K and emerge at L.

13. Pull the thread through. Work a stitch very close to the previous stitch.

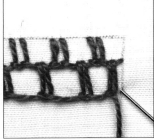

14. Continue working pairs of stitches to the opposite side of the shape. Take the thread to the back at the side of the shape and secure.

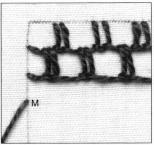

15. Bring the thread to the front at M.

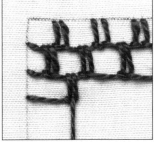

16. Work a pair of stitches as before, positioning the vertical sections directly below those in the first row.

17. Continue to the end of the row, positioning the pairs of stitches directly below those in the first row.

18. Continue working rows until the shape is filled.

BONNET STITCH

This stitch is worked from right to left in a line. The stitch can be widely spaced to create a lacy line or worked closely to form a heavy line.

1. Bring the thread to the front at A.

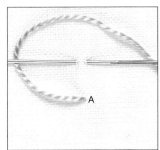

2. Make a small horizontal stitch directly above A. Ensure that the thread is under the tip of the needle.

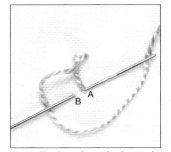

3. Pull the thread through. Make a small angled stitch from A to B. Ensure the thread is under the tip of the needle.

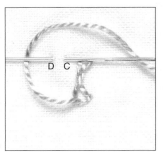

4. Loop the thread as shown. Make a small horizontal stitch from C to D. Ensure thread is under the tip of the needle.

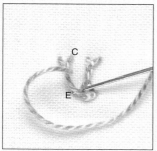

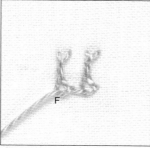

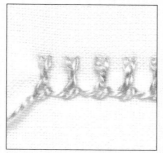

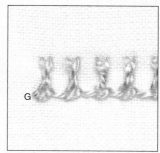

5. Take the needle to the back at E, directly below C and over the loop of thread.

6. Emerge at F. Ensure the thread is under the tip of the needle. Pull the thread through.

7. Continue working in this manner to the end of the line.

8. To end off, take the needle to the back at G and secure.

BRETON STITCH

This is a wide border stitch, worked between two lines. The stitches overlap along the lower edge and sit side-by-side along the upper edge. Mark temporary parallel lines onto the fabric.

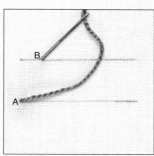

1. Bring the thread to the front at A. Take the needle to the back at B.

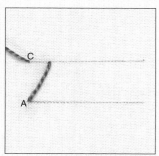

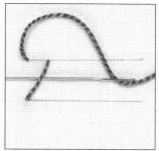

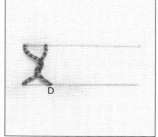

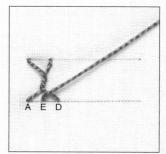

2. Pull the thread through keeping the stitch relaxed. Emerge at C, directly above A.

3. Slide the needle, from right to left, under the stitch.

4. Take the needle to the back at D. Pull the thread through.

5. Emerge at E on the lower line, halfway between A and D.

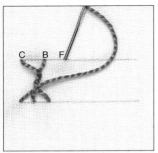 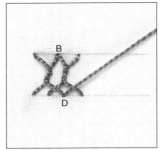 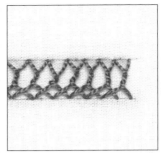 

6. Take the needle to the back at F. The distance between B and F must be the same as B and C.

7. Emerge at B, through the same hole in the fabric. Complete the second stitch following steps 3 and 4. Emerge at D.

8. Continue in this manner to the end of the row, ensuring the spacing of the stitches is kept even.

9. To work along a curved line, work the stitches slightly wider along the outer edge of the curve.

BURDEN STITCH COUCHING

This is an effective filling stitch that can be used on most shapes.
The couching stitches are the same length as the space between the laid threads.

 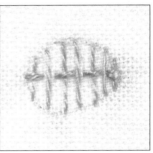

1. Work the vertical laid threads.

2. Couch the centre of each alternate laid thread, taking each stitch through the fabric.

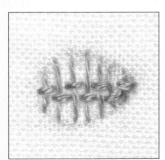 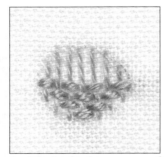 

3. Couch a second row below the previous row in a similar manner.

4. Work further rows of couching below the second row, reducing the number of stitches to fill the shape.

5. Complete the remaining half of the shape in the same manner.

CABLE STITCH — DOUBLE

Double cable stitch is worked as two adjacent rows of cable stitch.
One edge of the second row is worked in the same holes as the first row.

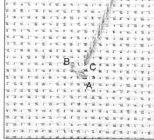

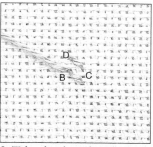

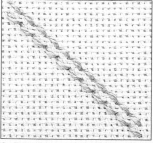

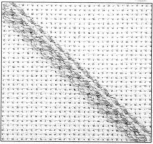

1. Bring the thread to the front at A. Take to the back at B, two threads above and to the left of A. Emerge at C, two threads above A.

2. Take the thread to the back at D, two threads above and to the left of C. Emerge at B.

3. Repeat steps 1 and 2 along the row.

4. Work another row of cable adjacent to the first row. The stitches in the middle share the same holes.

CABLE CHAIN STITCH

This is a variation of chain stitch that forms a row of chains linked by straight stitches. The chains should be slightly longer than the stitches between them. Mark a temporary line onto the fabric.

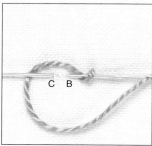

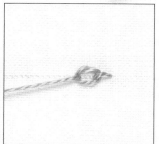

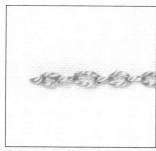

1. Bring the thread to the front at A. Wrap the thread around the needle as shown.

2. Pull thread firmly around the needle. Insert the needle at B and emerge at C, keeping the thread under the tip of the needle.

3. Keeping the thread taut around the needle, pull through to form the first cable chain stitch.

4. Continue working in this manner to the end of the row.

5. To end off, anchor the last chain with a straight stitch. Secure the thread at the back.

CABLE PLAIT STITCH

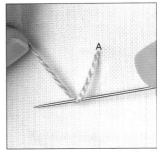

1. Bring the thread to the front at A. Loop the thread over the needle as shown.

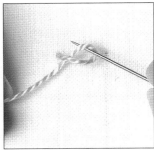

2. Twist the tip of the needle back over the thread in a counter-clockwise direction.

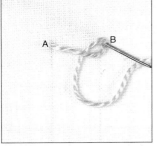

3. Keeping the loop on the needle, take the needle to the back at B.

4. Pull the thread through, leaving a loop on the front.

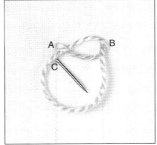

5. Bring the needle to the front at C, inside the new loop and below A.

6. Pull the loop taut around the tip of the needle.

7. Pull the thread through.

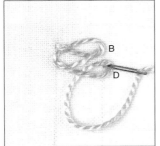

8. Hold the thread to the left. Repeat steps 1 - 3, taking the needle to the back at D below B.

9. Repeat steps 4 - 7 to complete the stitch in the same manner as before.

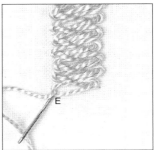

10. Continue working in the same manner. To finish, take the needle to the back at E and secure.

CAST-ON STITCH

This stitch is commonly used in Brazilian embroidery and is similar in appearance to a detached blanket stitch bar. It can be used to form dainty flowers in much the same way as bullion knots. Work this stitch with a milliner's needle.

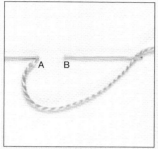

1. Bring the thread to the front at A. Take the thread to the back at B and emerge as close as possible to A. Leave the needle in the fabric.

2. Slide one finger beneath the emerging thread as shown.

3. Rotate your finger towards you, keeping the thread taut.

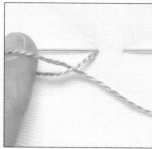

4. Keeping the tension on the thread, place your finger tip on the point of the needle.

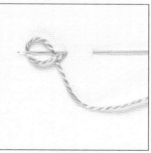

5. Slip the loop off your finger and onto the needle.

6. Pull the thread tight and slip the loop down the needle as shown.

7. Work a second cast-on in the same manner.

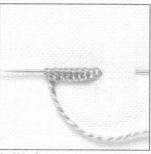

8. Work as many cast-ons as required.

9. Holding the cast-ons, pull the needle and thread through the stitches.

10. Tighten the thread, allowing the stitch to flip to the right.

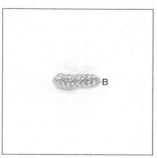

11. To end off, take the needle to the back close to B and secure.

CAST-ON STITCH — DOUBLE

This stitch is always worked with two strands of thread in the needle.

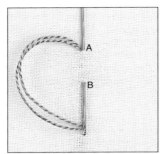

1. Bring the thread to the front at A. Take a stitch from B to A leaving the needle in the fabric.

2. Separate the two strands and place one each side of the needle.

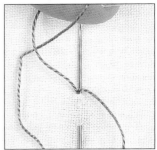

3. Twist the left thread into a loop around your finger. Place your fingertip on the point of the needle.

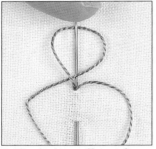

4. Slip the loop off your finger and onto the needle.

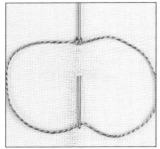

5. Slip the loop down the needle onto the fabric and pull tight.

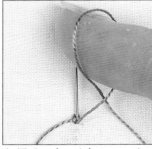

6. Twist the right emerging thread around your finger in the same manner.

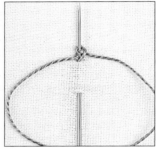

7. Slip the loop onto the needle, positioning it next to the first, and pull tight.

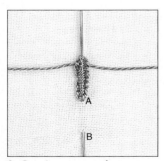

8. Continue to work cast-ons alternating from side to side matching the distance from A to B.

9. Hold the cast-ons and pull the needle and thread through the stitches.

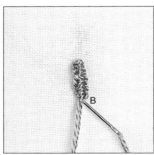

10. To anchor the stitch, take the needle to the back at B.

CHAIN STITCH – BACK STITCH COMBINATION

This stitch combination is effective for adding texture to borders and lines.

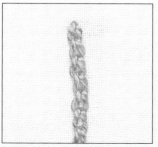 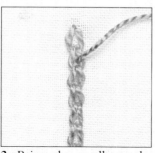 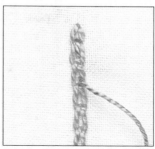 

1. Work a row of chain stitch as a foundation.

2. Bring the needle to the front, inside the second chain stitch. Pull the thread through.

3. Take the needle to the back, through the first chain stitch and emerge in the third chain stitch. Pull through.

4. Continue working back stitch into the chain stitches along the entire row.

CHAIN STITCH – CRESTED

Also known as Spanish coral stitch, crested chain forms a wide, lacy line varying in effect according to how closely the stitches are worked. If working on finely woven fabric, mark two temporary guidelines.

1. Bring the thread to the front at A. Work a small chain stitch.

2. Form a loop in the thread as shown.

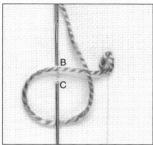 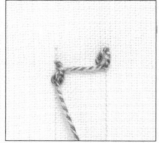 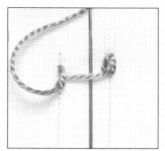 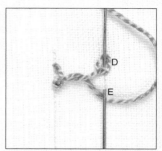

3. Take the needle from B to C. Ensure the needle goes beneath the top part of the loop but over the lower part.

4. Pull the thread through, forming a second chain stitch.

5. Slide the needle behind the connecting thread and pull through. Do not go through the fabric.

6. Take the needle from D to E. Ensure that the thread is under the tip of the needle.

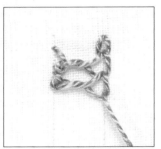  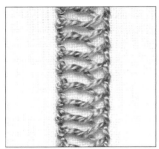 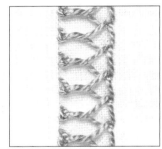

7. Pull the thread through. Repeat the sequence from step 2.

8. Continue working to the end of the line.

9. Closed crested chain.

10. Open crested chain.

CHAIN STITCH — DOUBLE

This is a simple variation of chain stitch and is also known as Türkmen stitch. If working on finely woven fabric, mark two temporary guidelines.

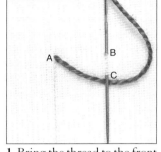 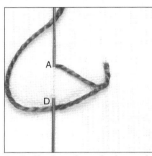

1. Bring the thread to the front at A. Take the needle to the back at B and emerge at C. Ensure that the thread is under the tip of the needle.

2. Pull the thread through. Loop the thread as shown. Take the needle to the back at A and emerge at D. Ensure that the thread is under the tip of the needle.

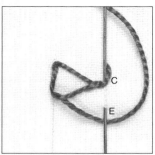 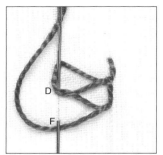 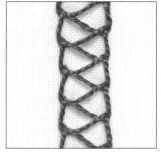 

3. Pull the thread through. Take the needle to the back at C and emerge at E. Ensure that the thread is under the tip of the needle.

4. Pull the thread through. Loop the thread as shown. Take the needle to the back at D and emerge at F. Ensure that the thread is under the tip of the needle.

5. Pull through. Continue working in this manner along the lines.

6. To end off, take the thread to the back over the last loop worked and secure.

CHAIN STITCH — DOUBLE DETACHED

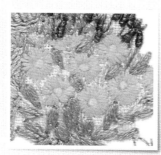

Also known as berry stitch, it can be used to embroider leaves, buds and flower petals. It is created by working a detached chain, then stitching another slightly larger detached chain, around the first. The stitch can be worked in two colours.

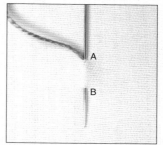

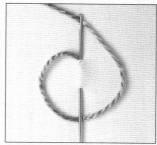

1. Bring the thread to the front at A. Take the needle to the back through the same hole and emerge at B.

2. Loop the thread under the tip of the needle as shown.

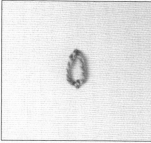

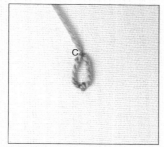

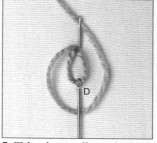

3. Pull the thread through. To anchor the stitch, take the needle to the back over the loop.

4. Bring the thread to the front at C.

5. Take the needle to the back through the same hole. Emerge at D. Ensure the thread is under the tip of the needle.

6. Pull the thread through and anchor the stitch.

CHAIN STITCH — HEAVY

This stitch produces a thick braided line. The thickness is achieved by taking the needle under two chain stitch loops to form each stitch. Mark a guideline onto the fabric.

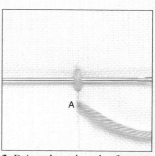

1. Bring the thread to the front at the top of the line and work a small straight stitch.

2. Bring thread to the front at A. Slide the needle, from right to left, under the straight stitch. Do not go through the fabric.

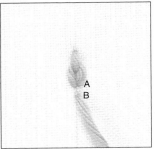

3. Take the thread to the back at A to form a chain stitch and emerge at B.

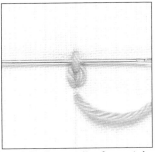

4. Slide the needle, from right to left, under the straight stitch.

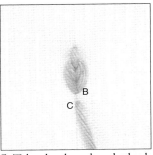

5. Take the thread to the back at B to form a chain. Emerge at C.

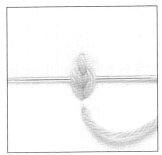

6. Slide the needle behind the two previous chain stitches.

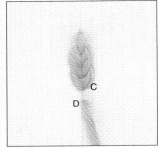

7. Take the thread to the back at C to form a chain. Emerge at D.

8. Slide the needle behind the two previous chain stitches and take the thread to the back at D.

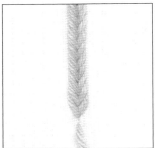

9. Continue working in this manner, sliding the needle behind the two previous stitches each time.

10. To end off, take the needle to the back to form the last chain and secure.

CHAIN STITCH — HUNGARIAN BRAIDED

This stitch is worked in a similar way to heavy chain but the thread is only taken under the first of the previous two chains.

1. Bring the thread to the front at the top of the line and work a small straight stitch.

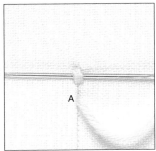

2. Bring the thread to the front at A. Slide the needle, from right to left, under the straight stitch. Do not go through the fabric.

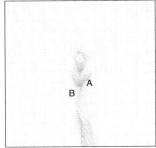

3. Take the thread to the back at A to form a chain stitch and emerge at B.

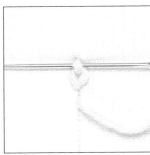

4. Slide the needle, from right to left, under the straight stitch.

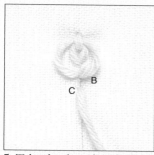

5. Take the thread to the back at B to form a loose chain. Emerge at C.

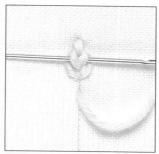

6. Slide the needle under the first chain only. Tighten the second loop.

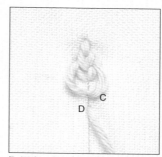

7. Take the thread to the back at C to form a loose chain and emerge at D.

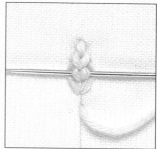

8. Slide the needle under the second chain only. Tighten the third loop.

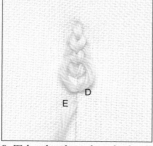

9. Take the thread to the back at D to form a loose chain and emerge at E.

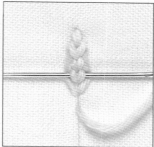

10. Slide the thread under the third chain only. Tighten the fourth loop.

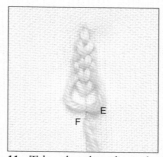

11. Take the thread to the back at E to form a chain and emerge at F.

12. Continue working in this manner to the end of the line.

CHAIN STITCH — KNOTTED

This stitch requires careful tensioning to obtain the correct results.
It is worked from right to left. Mark a line onto the fabric.

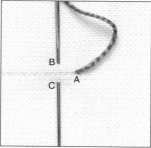

1. Bring the thread to the front at A. Take the needle to the back at B and emerge at C.

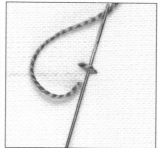

2. Pull the thread through. Loop the thread as shown. Slide the needle behind the diagonal stitch.

3. Pull the thread through. Slide the needle under the top of the loop, over the base and the working thread as shown.

4. Pull the thread through.

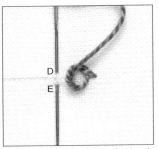   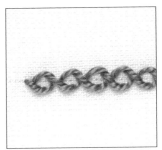

5. Take the needle to the back at D and emerge at E.

6. Pull the thread through. Loop the thread as shown and slide the needle behind the diagonal stitch.

7. Pull the thread through. Slide the needle under the top of the loop, over the base and the working thread as shown.

8. Pull the thread through. Repeat the stitch sequence to the end of the line.

CHAIN STITCH — KNOTTED CABLE

This stitch is a combination of coral stitch and chain stitch.

 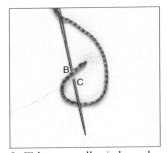  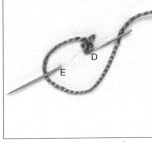

1. Bring the thread to the front at A on the line to be covered. Hold the thread in place along the line.

2. Take a small stitch under the line and the laid thread from B to C. The loop of the thread is under the tip of the needle.

3. Pull the thread through, making a coral knot. Slide the needle under the first stitch.

4. Loop the thread as shown. Take a stitch from D to E. Keep the thread under the tip of the needle.

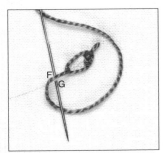  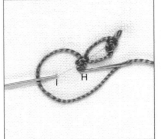 

5. Pull the thread through, making a chain. Take the needle from F to G, under the laid thread and over the loop.

6. Pull the thread through. Slide the needle under the stitch between the chain and the second knot.

7. Pull the thread through. Work a chain, taking the needle from H to I, keeping the thread under the tip of the needle.

8. Continue following steps 5 - 7. To end off, work a knot after the last chain and take needle to the back between the last knot and chain and secure.

CHAIN STITCH — WHIPPED REVERSE

It is essential to work with a firm thread to achieve the correct effect. A line of reverse chain stitch forms the foundation row.

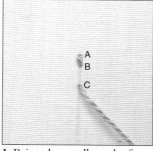

1. Bring the needle to the front at A. Take it to the back at B and emerge at C.

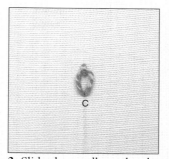

2. Slide the needle under the first stitch and take it to the back at C. Pull the thread through.

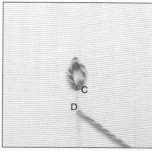

3. Bring the needle to the front at D.

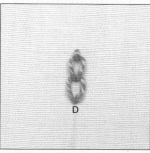

4. Slide the needle and thread under the first chain without catching the fabric. Take the thread to the back at D.

5. Continue stitching in this manner to the end of the row.

6. Using a second thread, bring the needle to the front inside the first chain on the design line.

7. Slide the needle under the left half of this chain. Do not go through the fabric.

8. Pull the thread through. Slide the needle from right to left under the second chain.

9. Pull the thread through until the whipped stitch rests gently against the chain stitch.

10. Continue in the same manner. To end off, take the thread to the back under the last chain.

CHAINED FEATHER STITCH

Also known as feathered chain stitch, this stitch has the appearance of a stem with tiny buds. Each stitch is worked as a detached chain. Mark temporary parallel guidelines onto the fabric.

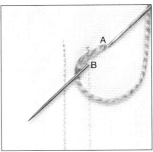

1. Bring the thread to the front at A. Take the needle from A to B, ensuring the thread is under the tip of the needle.

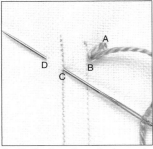

2. Pull the thread through. Take the needle from C to D. The distance from C to D should be the same as A to B.

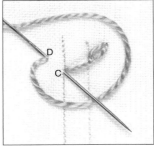

3. Insert the needle at D and emerge at C keeping the thread under the tip of the needle.

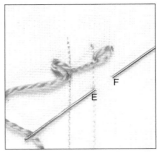

4. Pull the thread through. Insert the needle at E, directly below B and emerge at F, directly below A.

5. Continue in this manner to the end of the row. To end off, anchor the last chain with a straight stitch.

CHEVRON STITCH

This stitch is best worked between two parallel guidelines. Keep the needle parallel to the marked line for each stitch.

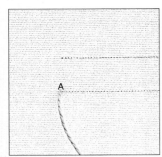

1. Bring the thread to the front at A on the left hand side of the lower line.

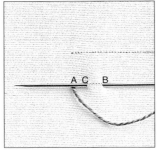

2. With the thread below the needle, take the needle to the back at B and emerge at C, halfway between A and B.

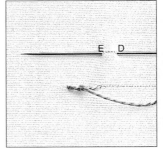

3. Pull the thread through. With the thread below, take the needle from D to E on the upper line.

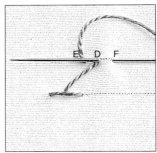

4. Pull the thread through. With the thread above, take the needle from F to D.

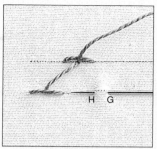
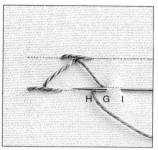
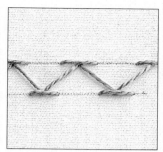

5. Pull through to form a straight stitch on the upper line. With the thread above, take the needle from G to H on the lower line.

6. Pull the thread through. With the thread below, take the needle from I to G.

7. Pull the thread through to form a straight stitch on the lower line. Continue working stitches between the lines in the same manner.

8. To work a curve, the stitches on the inside line are gradually shortened and positioned closer together.

CHEVRON STITCH — HALF

Half chevron stitch creates an attractive border with a solid lower line. It can also be used as an isolated motif. Mark a line onto the fabric.

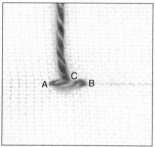

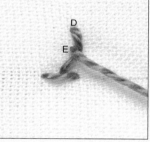

1. Bring the thread to the front at A. Take the thread to the back at B and emerge at C, halfway along the stitch.

2. Loop the thread as shown.

3. Take the needle to the back at D and emerge at E. Pull thread through ensuring that the thread is under the tip of the needle.

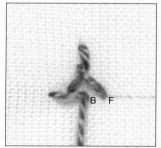
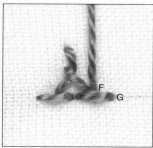

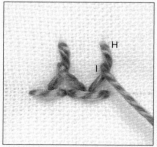

4. Take the needle to the back at F and emerge at B.

5. Take the needle to the back at G and emerge at F.

6. Loop the thread as shown.

7. Take the needle to the back at H and emerge at I. Pull thread through ensuring the thread is under the tip of the needle.

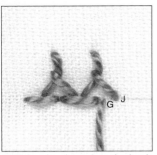  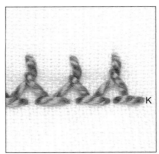 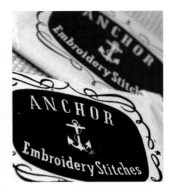

8. Take the thread to the back at J and emerge at G.

9. Continue working in this manner to the end of the row.

10. Take the thread to the back at K and secure.

CHEVRON STITCH — WHIPPED

An attractive border stitch, whipped chevron stitch can be worked in a single colour or a combination of colours to create a pretty effect. Use a tapestry needle to work the whipping stitches. Mark temporary parallel lines onto the fabric.

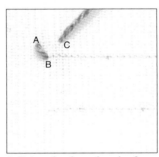 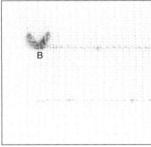

1. Bring the thread to the front at A. Take the thread to the back at B and emerge at C.

2. Take the thread to the back at B to form a 'V'.

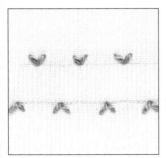 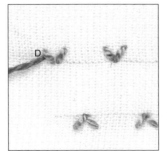 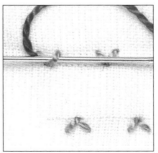 

3. Work regularly spaced 'V's along both lines, offsetting the second line and inverting the 'V' shapes.

4. Bring the whipping thread to the surface at D.

5. With the thread above the needle, slide the needle, from right to left, under the stitch as shown.

6. With the thread above, slide the needle, from right to left, under the stitch as shown.

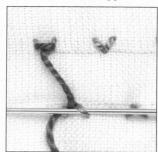

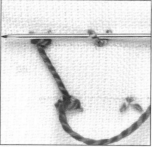

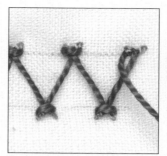

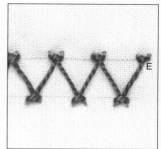

7. With the thread below, slide the needle under the second half of the lower 'V'.

8. With the thread beneath the needle, slide the needle under the first half of the next 'V' on the top line.

9. Continue to work in this manner to the end of the lines.

10. Take the thread to the back at E and secure.

CHINESE KNOT

This stitch makes a wonderfully textured line and can be used as a single line or as a filling stitch.
Mark parallel guidelines onto the fabric.

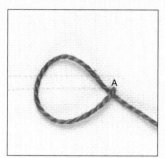

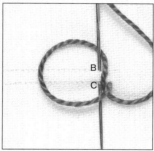

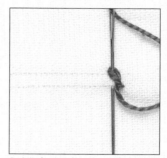

1. Bring the thread to the front at A. Create a loop in the thread as shown.

2. Insert the needle at B, inside the loop and emerge at C. The needle should be over the top of the loop and under the base of the loop.

3. Tighten the thread so that the loop is sitting firmly around the needle.

4. Pull the thread through.

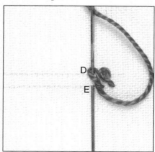

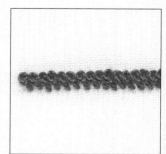

5. Create a loop in the thread as shown.

6. Insert the needle at D and emerge at E. Tighten the thread around the needle.

7. Pull the thread through.

8. Continue working in this manner to the end of the row.

CHINESE KNOT VARIATION

This variation creates a row of circles, each one linked with a small stitch.
It differs from the Chinese knot in the positioning of the lower thread in relation to the
needle when forming the knot. This creates an open stitch rather than a tight knot.

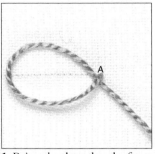

1. Bring the thread to the front at A. Create a loop in the thread as shown.

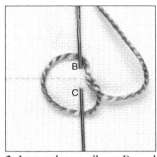

2. Insert the needle at B, and emerge at C. Both the top and the base of the loop should be under the needle.

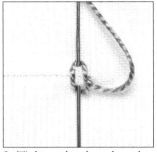

3. Tighten the thread so that the loop is sitting firmly around the needle.

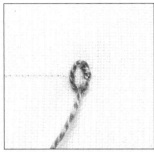

4. Pull the thread through.

5. Take the thread to the back just over the base of the loop.

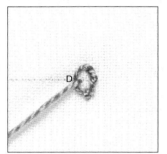

6. Bring the thread to the front at D, just inside the loop.

7. Create a loop in the thread as shown.

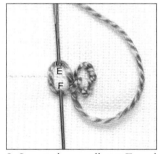

8. Insert the needle at E and emerge at F. Both the top and the base of the loop should be under the needle. Tighten the loop.

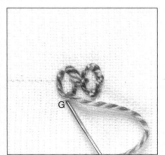

9. Pull the thread through and take the needle to the back at G.

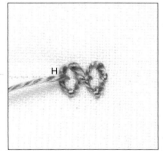

10. Emerge at H.

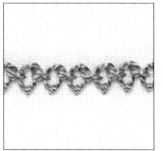

11. Continue working in this manner to the end of the row.

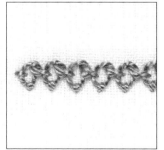

12. Take the thread to the back over the loop and secure.

COLONIAL KNOT — RUNNING STITCH

Running stitches are combined with a colonial knot to create this ingenious rose.

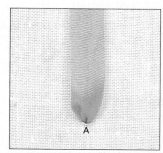

1. Bring the ribbon to the front of the fabric at A.

2. Wrap the ribbon around the needle as if making a colonial knot, approx 5 - 6cm (2 - 2 3/8") from the fabric.

3. Take 6 - 8 running stitches, each approx 6mm (1/4") long, down the centre of the ribbon.

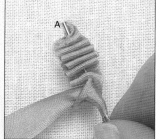

4. Insert the needle into the fabric close to A. Tighten the knot. Begin to push the needle through to the back of the fabric.

5. Pull through until the ribbon folds up into petals with the colonial knot in the centre.

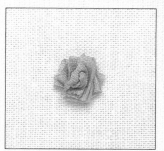

6. End off on the back of the fabric. Adjust the petals with the eye of the needle.

CORAL STITCH — CORDED

1. Secure the thread and bring it to the front at the right hand side of the line to be covered.

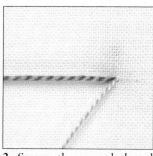

2. Secure the second thread and bring it to the front at the same position.

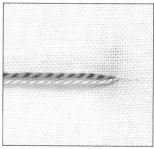

3. Lay the threads along the line and hold in place.

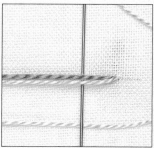

4. Take a tiny stitch under the threads and through the fabric. Keep the working thread below needle.

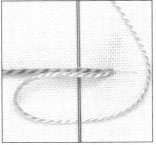

5. Hold the laid thread along the line and begin to pull the working thread through.

6. Continue to pull gently to form a coral stitch around the laid thread.

7. Work a second coral stitch.

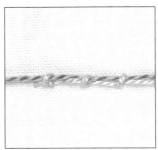

8. Continue in this manner to the end of the row.

CORAL STITCH VARIATION

This interesting variation of coral stitch is worked in a similar way to coral or coral knot stitch. Here the stitch is worked inside a loop formed by the working thread, rather than over the working thread. Mark a line onto the fabric.

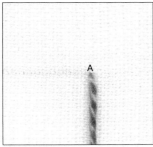

1. Bring the thread to the front at A.

2. Loop the thread as shown.

3. Make a small stitch inside the loop.

4. Pull the thread through to form a tight knot.

coral stitch variation | *continued*

5. Loop the thread as shown.

6. Make a small stitch inside the loop.

7. Pull the thread through to form a tight knot.

8. Continue working in this manner to the end of the line. Take the thread to the back and secure.

CORD STITCH

This stitch produces a firm, dense edging and can be used to create a line of colour on the edge of fabric.

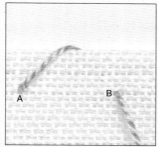

1. Bring the thread to the front at A. Take the thread over the edge and emerge at B.

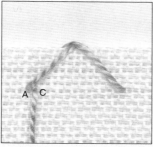

2. Take the thread over the edge and emerge at C, to the right of A.

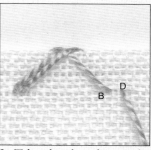

3. Take the thread over the edge and emerge at D, to the right of B.

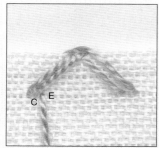

4. Take the thread over the edge and emerge at E, to the right of C.

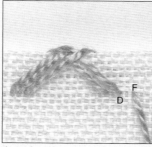

5. Take the thread over the edge and emerge at F, to the right of D.

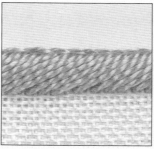

6. Continue working in this manner to the end of the line.

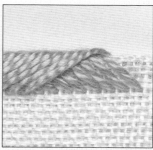

7. Take the thread to the back and secure.

COUCHING — PUFFY

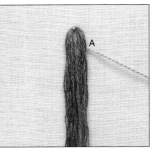

1. Fold a bundle of strands in half. Secure the fold. Carefully comb the threads to form a smooth bundle.

2. Lay foundation threads along the design line. Bring the couching thread to the front on the line at A.

3. Take the thread to the back on the design line at B, forming a very short straight stitch.

4. Lift the foundation threads with a tapestry needle to puff the threads.

5. Continue couching the foundation threads, lifting each section to achieve a puffed effect.

6. To end off, sink the foundation threads to the back of work and secure.

CRETAN STITCH — SLANTED

This delicate filling stitch is also known as long armed feather stitch.

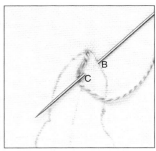

1. Secure the thread on the back of the fabric and bring it to the front at A.

2. Take the needle from B to C, ensuring the thread is under the tip of the needle.

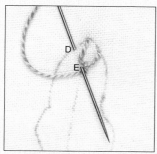  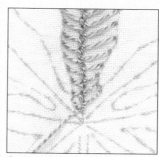 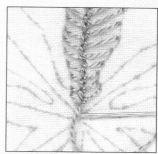

3. Pull the thread through. Take the needle from D to E, ensuring the thread is under the tip of the needle.

4. Pull the thread through until it lies snugly against the emerging thread.

5. Continue stitching in the same manner, alternating from right to left.

6. To finish, take the needle to the back of the fabric below the last stitch, close to where it emerged and secure.

CROSS STITCH — CHAINED

This variation of cross stitch has a detached chain crossing a diagonal stitch. Unlike basic cross stitch, each stitch must be fully worked before commencing the next stitch. If working on closely woven fabric, draw temporary parallel guidelines onto the fabric.

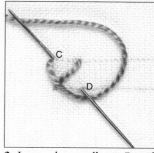

1. Bring the thread to the front at A. Take the thread to the back at B and emerge at C.

2. Insert the needle at C and emerge at D ensuring that the thread is under the tip of the needle.

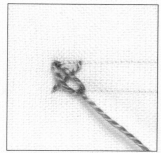 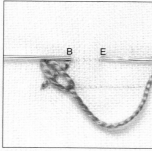  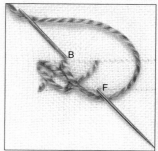

3. Pull the thread through.

4. Insert the needle at E and emerge at B.

5. Pull the thread through.

6. Insert the needle at B and emerge at F ensuring that the thread is under the tip of the needle.

 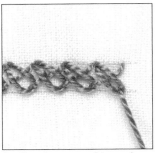  

7. Pull the thread through.

8. Continue working along the line in this manner.

9. To end off, take the thread to the back over the loop of the last chain and secure.

CROSS STITCH — RAISED

The arrow indicates the top of the fabric.

 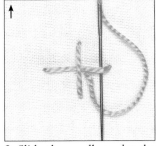  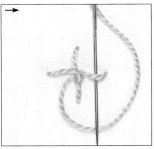

1. Work an upright cross stitch. Bring the needle to the front at A, below and to the right of the cross.

2. Slide the needle under the right spoke, without picking up any fabric. Keep the thread under the needle tip.

3. Pull the thread through around the spoke of the cross.

4. Turn the fabric 90 degrees to the right. Take the needle under the next spoke in the same manner.

 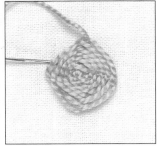

5. Work over the remaining spokes, turning the fabric for each stitch. Ensure the stitches lie snugly around the centre.

6. Continue in this manner around the spokes until the cross is covered. Take the needle under the shape and secure at the back.

Fabrics

Almost any type of fabric is suitable for embroidery. It is important to keep in mind, however, that in most cases the fabric will show through the stitches.

When choosing your fabric consider it in relation to the threads you intend to use. The weight and weave of the fabric will need to be able to support the weight of the stitches. Lightweight fabrics usually combine well with finer threads.

It is a good idea to work a small sample on a spare piece of fabric to ensure the fabric, threads and stitches you are about to use will give you the result you are looking for.

CROSS STITCH — WOVEN

Woven cross stitch can be used as a continual line or as a scattered or dense filling stitch. Try working the second cross in a different colour for a pretty effect.

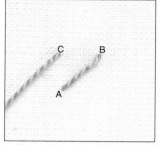

1. Bring thread to the surface at A. Take the thread to the back at B and emerge at C.

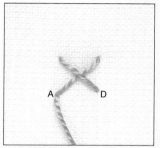

2. Take the thread to the back at D and emerge at A.

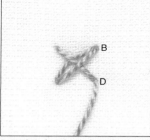

3. Take the thread to the back at B and emerge at D.

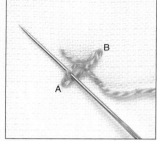

4. Take the needle over the lower thread between A and B and under the upper thread between A and B.

5. Insert the needle at C.

6. Pull the thread through.

DEERFIELD HERRINGBONE STITCH

This textured variation of herringbone stitch can be worked as a filling stitch or as a border of line stitch. The thread junctions formed at the upper and lower edges of the stitch are anchored by small straight stitches. Anchor all the upper stitch junctions before working the lower junctions to keep the back of the work neat.

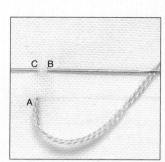

1. Bring the thread to the front at A. With the thread below, take the needle from B to C.

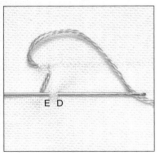

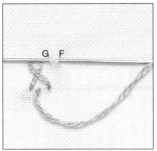

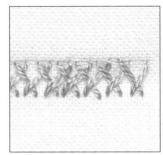

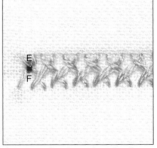

2. Pull the thread through. With the thread above, take the needle from D to E.

3. Pull the thread through. With the thread below, take the needle from F to G.

4. Continue working evenly spaced stitches across the row.

5. Bring the thread to the front at E. Take the needle to the back at F, moving the thread junction towards E.

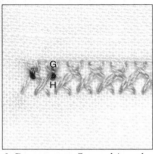

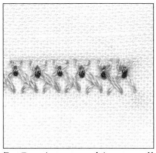

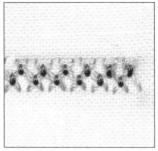

6. Repeat step 5, working the small anchoring stitch from G to H.

7. Continue working small anchoring stitches across the herringbone stitch junctions near the upper outline.

8. Work the anchoring stitches close to the lower outline in the same manner.

Blue and white are the characteristic colours of **Deerfield embroidery,** a style of stitching that has its origins in Deerfield, Massachusetts, USA. The Deerfield society of Blue and White Needlework was started in 1898 to preserve and revive embroidery of the Colonial period.

DETACHED NEEDLELACE

Use a contrasting colour to couch the wire in place. Begin and end threads by sliding under the couching stitches and the wire edge. These threads will be enclosed and secured by the blanket stitch that is worked over the wire after the needlelace is complete. The couching stitches are the only stitches that go through the fabric.

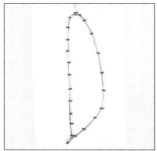

1. Leaving a small tail at both ends, couch the wire around the outline. Use tweezers to pinch the wire together to create a tip.

2. Secure the thread on the left hand edge of the shape. Work enough blanket stitches over the wire to cover the top of the shape. Do not go through the fabric.

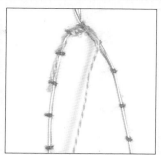

3. Wrap the thread twice around the wire on the right hand side.

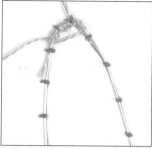

4. Slide the needle under the wire on the left hand side then wrap around the wire twice.

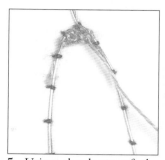

5. Using the loops of the previous row and the laid thread, work a second row of detached blanket stitches.

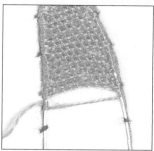

6. Continue working in this manner, increasing as necessary by adding a new stitch at the beginning, and if required, the end of the row.

7. As the shape begins to narrow, decrease by omitting a stitch at the beginning, and if necessary, the end of the row.

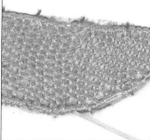

8. Beginning at the top of the shape, work close blanket stitch over the wire.

9. At the tip, wrap the thread tightly around the wire to cover it.

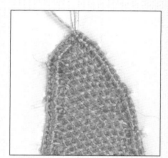

10. Continue working blanket stitch until reaching the starting point.

11. At the back of the fabric, cut away the couching stitches.

12. Remove the lace from the fabric.

DIAGONAL CHEVRON STITCH

This is a pulled thread stitch and creates a strong, ridged, diagonal pattern. Pull each stitch firmly to open the fabric threads. It is best worked on even weave fabric.

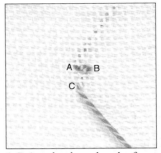

1. Bring the thread to the front at A. Take it to the back at B and emerge at C.

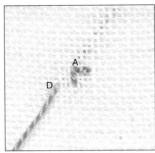

2. Take the thread to the back at A and emerge at D.

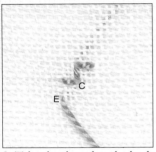

3. Take the thread to the back at C and emerge at E.

4. Continue working in this manner for the required distance.

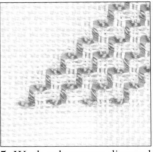

5. Work subsequent diagonal lines, each one, three fabric threads from the previous row as shown.

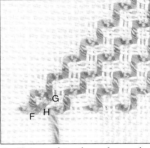

6. Bring the thread to the surface at F. Take it to the back at G and emerge at H.

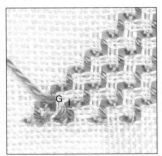

7. Take the thread to the back at I and emerge at G.

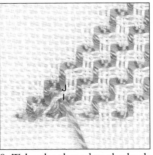

8. Take the thread to the back at J and emerge at I.

9. Continue working in this manner, using the same holes as the first pass.

Pulled Thread Embroidery takes its name from stitches that are worked with tension into open, even weave fabric, pulling the fabric threads to create an open, lacy effect.

An even weave fabric has to be used to produce an even look to the pulled stitches.

As a rule, the embroidery thread used should be the same thickness as the fabric threads themselves.

DIAGONAL DRAWN FILLING STITCH

This is a simple pulled thread stitch, requiring only one thread pass for each row. Each subsequent row is set one stitch below and one stitch to the right of the previous row. Pull each stitch firmly to open the fabric threads.

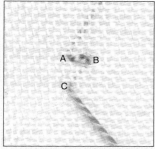

1. Bring the thread to the front at A. Take it to the back at B and emerge at C.

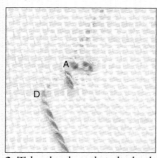

2. Take the thread to the back at A and emerge at D.

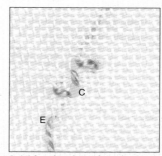

3. Take the thread to the back at C and emerge at E.

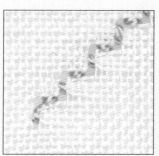

4. Continue working in this manner for the required distance.

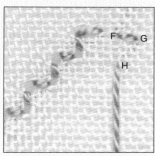

5. Bring the thread to the front at F, Take it to the back at G and emerge at H.

6. Take the thread to the back at F and emerge at I.

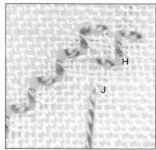

7. Take the thread to the back at H and emerge at J.

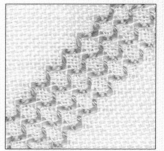

8. Continue working rows in this manner.

DIAGONAL RAISED BAND STITCH

This is a form of pulled thread cross stitch, creating a trellis of upright crosses. Pull each stitch firmly to open the fabric threads and form the characteristic ridges in the fabric. Here the stitch is worked over a block of six fabric threads and each stitch moves half this distance (three threads) from the last.

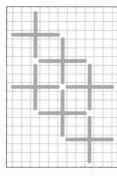

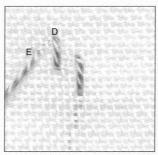

1. Bring the thread to the surface at A. Take it to the back at B and emerge at C.

2. Take the thread to the back at D and emerge at E.

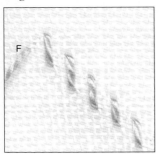 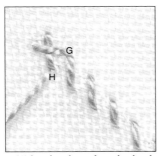  

3. Continue working in this manner the required distance. Bring the thread to the front at F.

4. Take the thread to the back at G and emerge at H.

5. Continue working in this manner to the end of the row.

6. Continue working rows in the same manner, sharing holes from the previous rows.

DIAMOND FILLING STITCH

This pulled thread stitch is worked as double rows of back stitch to form a line of diamonds. Pull each stitch firmly to open the fabric threads and enhance the pattern.

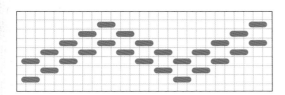

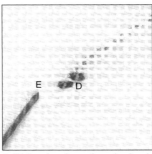

1. Bring the thread to the front at A. Take the thread to the back at B and emerge at C.

2. Take the thread to the back at D and emerge at E.

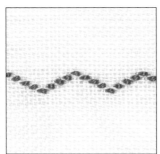  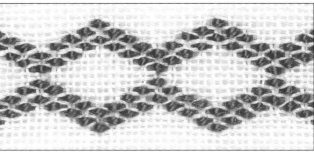

3. Continue working in this manner, forming a zigzag line.

4. Work a second zigzag row, leaving two free threads between the points.

5. Work mirror image rows to form a lattice.

DIAMOND STITCH

Perfect for stitching open borders, diamond stitch can also be worked in parallel rows to create a pretty filling. Mark temporary parallel lines onto the fabric.

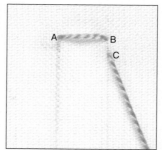

1. Bring the thread to the front at A. Take the thread to the back at B and emerge at C.

2. Make a loop in the working thread as shown.

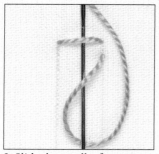

3. Slide the needle, from top to bottom, under the straight stitch, under and over the working thread as shown.

4. Pull the thread through and to the right to tighten the knot.

5. Make a loop as shown.

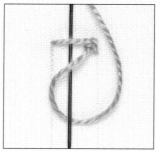

6. Slide the needle, from top to bottom, under the left end of the straight stitch, under and over the working thread as shown.

7. Pull the thread through and to the left to tighten the knot.

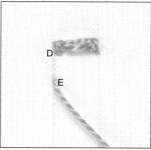

8. Take the thread to the back at D, directly under the knot, and emerge at E.

9. Make a loop as shown.

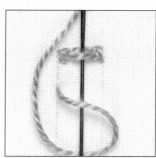

10. Slide the needle, from top to bottom, under the straight stitch, under and over the working thread.

11. Pull thread through and tighten the knot.

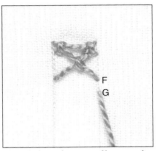

12. Take the needle to the back at F and emerge at G.

13. Make a loop as shown.

14. Slide the needle, from top to bottom, under the stitch, under and over the working thread.

15. Pull the thread through and to the right to tighten the knot.

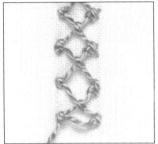

16. Continue working in this manner to the end of the lines.

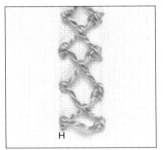

17. Take the thread to the back at H and secure on the back.

DORSET BUTTON

A metal ring or washer is covered with wool or heavy cotton, then woven in patterns to fill the central hole. Changing colour adds to the effect. When weaving through the threads at the back to finish off, a thread can be left for attaching to a garment.

1. Casting. Tie the thread to the ring. Work detached blanket stitch closely around the ring, securing the tail under the stitches.

2. Slicking. Push the purl of the stitches to the inside of the ring. The working thread is now inside the ring.

3. Laying. With the thread at the top, wind it over the opposite side of the ring and back to the top, ending very slightly to the right.

4. Wind a second time, with the thread slightly to the right at the top and to the left at the opposite side.

  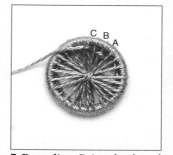 

5. Turning the ring slightly, continue winding until the space is completely covered.

6. Take the thread to the centre at the back. Work several cross stitches exactly at the centre, to firmly fix the threads.

7. Rounding. Bring the thread to the front at A. Take it to back at B and emerge at C, working the stitch over the front and back spokes.

8. Continue working stitches, over front and back threads, for two rounds. Secure on the back.

DOUBLE FAGGOT FILLING STITCH

A solid filling stitch, it creates a dense trellis and is worked onto even weave fabrics with easily counted threads. Pull each stitch firmly to open the fabric threads.

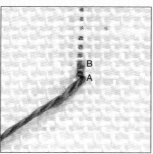 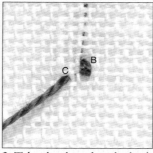 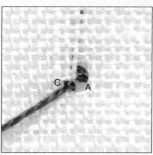

1. Bring the thread to the front at A. Take the thread to the back at B and re-emerge at A.

2. Take the thread to the back at B and emerge at C.

3. Take the thread to the back at A and re-emerge at C.

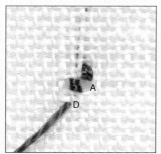   

4. Take the thread to the back at A and emerge at D.

5. Continue working in this manner to the end of the row.

6. Turn the fabric and work a second row of stitches, two threads to the right of the first row and sharing some of the same holes as the first row.

7. Continue working the two rows until the shape is filled.

DOUBLE PEKINESE STITCH

Ruling lines on the fabric will help keep the stitches straight and even.
Use very long threads for the weaving as it is
difficult to conceal a join. In the foundation ensure each backstitch of the second row is positioned directly above a stitch of the first row. At the outer corners, work an additional three slightly longer stitches either side of the corner.

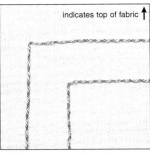

indicates top of fabric

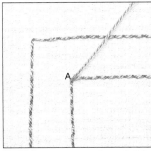

A

1. Work a row of back stitches for the inner foundation row. Work a second row approx 7mm (¹/₄") beyond the first.

2. Using a new thread (the weaving thread), bring the thread to the front at A, at the left hand side of the inner row of back stitches.

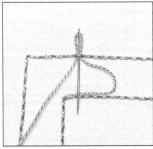

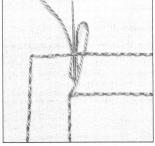

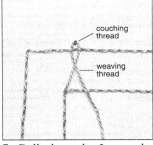

couching thread

weaving thread

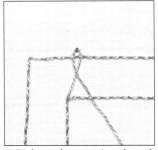

3. Slide the needle from bottom to the top under the fifth back stitch of the outer row. The needle does not go through the fabric.

4. Pull the thread through. Slide the needle from the top to the bottom under the fourth back stitch of the outer row.

5. Pull through. Leave the loop at the top. Bring the second thread to the front inside the loop. Couch with a tiny straight stitch. Leave couching thread on the back.

6. Pick up the weaving thread. Slide the needle from top to bottom under the third back stitch of the inner row. Pull the thread through.

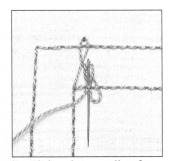

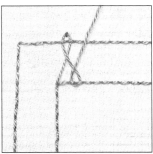

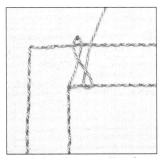

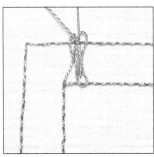

7. Slide the needle from bottom to top under the second back stitch of the inner row.

8. Pull the thread through until the loop rests gently against the lower edge of the back stitches.

9. Slide the needle from bottom to top under the sixth back stitch of the outer row. Pull the thread through.

10. Slide the needle from top to bottom under the fifth back stitch of the outer row.

11. Pull through leaving a tiny loop. Couch the loop in place with the second needle and thread.

12. Slide the weaving thread from top to bottom under the fourth back stitch of the inner row. Pull the thread through.

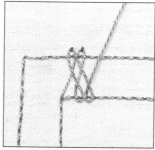

13. Slide the needle from bottom to top under the third back stitch of the inner row. Pull the thread through.

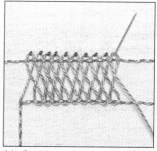

14. Continue working stitches in the same manner, couching each loop formed on the outer edge.

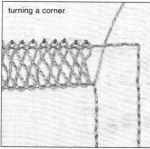

turning a corner

15. Take thread from top to bottom under the last inner back stitch before the corner. Slide the needle under the next outer back stitch. Pull through.

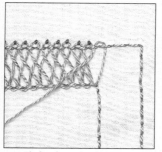

16. Slide the needle from top to bottom under the previous used back stitch of the outer row. Pull the thread through leaving a tiny loop at the outer edge.

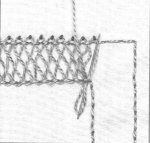

17. Couch the loop in place with a straight stitch. Slide the needle from the top to the bottom under the last back stitch of the inner row.

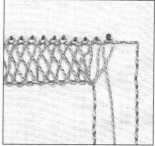

18. Pull the thread through. Form a loop between the second and third to last back stitches from the corner. Couch in place with a French knot.

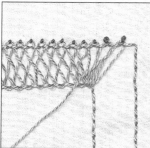

19. Work another stitch in the same manner between the inner and outer rows taking the thread under the last back stitch of the inner row as before.

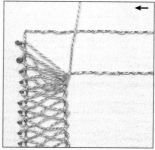

20. Rotate the fabric. Slide the needle from bottom to top under the first stitch after the the corner on the inner edge. Pull the thread through.

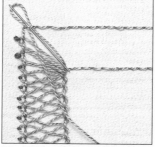

21. Slide the needle from bottom to top under the first back stitch after the corner of the outer row.

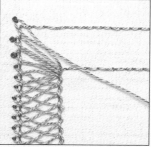

22. Pull the thread through. Slide the thread from top to bottom under the last back stitch before the corner, leaving a loop. Couch the loop with a French knot.

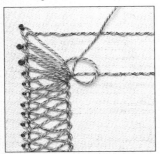

23. Slide the thread under the last back stitch of the inner row and then under the first back stitch past the corner of the inner row.

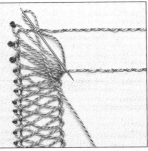

24. Slide the needle under the second back stitch past the corner of the outer row.

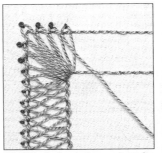

25. Work 3 stitches using the first back stitch past the corner of the inner row for each stitch. Couch the first 2 loops with French knots and the third with a straight stitch.

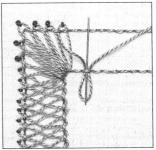

26. To begin the next straight section, slide the thread from top to bottom under the third back stitch of the inner row.

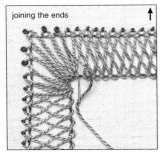

joining the ends

27. Continue working all sides in the same manner until you reach the first stitch. Take the thread to the back under the previous back stitch on the inner row and secure.

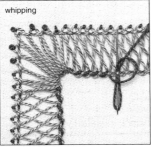

whipping

28. Whip the entire inner row, sliding the whipping stitches from top to bottom under each back stitch.

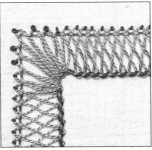

29. At the corners slide the whipping thread behind the weaving stitches.

DRAWN FAGGOT FILLING STITCH

This stitch creates an open, lacy pattern and is worked onto even weave fabrics with easily counted threads. The small squares are worked over two threads and the large squares are worked over four threads. Pull each stitch firmly to open the fabric holes.

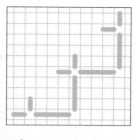

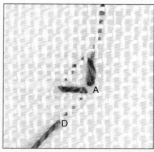

1. Bring the thread to the front at A. Take the thread to the back at B and emerge at C.

2. Take the thread to the back at A and emerge at D.

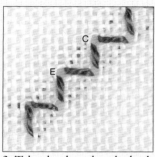

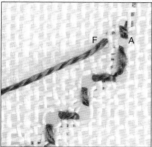

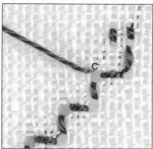

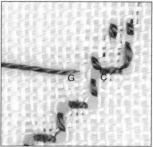

3. Take the thread to the back at C and emerge at E. Continue working in this manner to the end of the row.

4. Bring the thread to the front at A. Take the thread to the back two threads directly above. Emerge at F.

5. Take the thread to the back two threads directly above and emerge at C.

6. Take the thread to the back two threads directly above C and emerge at G.

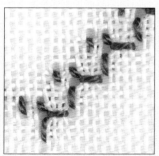

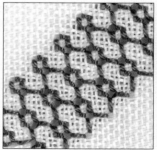

7. Continue working in this manner to the end of the row.

8. Turn the fabric and work pairs of stitches to complete the small squares.

9. Repeat the sequence of three rows until the desired shape is filled.

DRIZZLE STITCH

Drizzle stitch is a Brazilian embroidery stitch, best worked with a milliner's needle. It is created from cast-ons like those used in cast-on stitch.

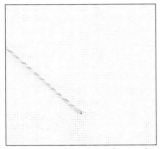

1. Secure the thread on the back of the fabric and bring it to the front.

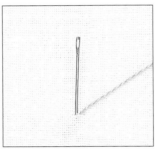

2. Unthread the needle. Insert the needle halfway into the fabric very close to where the thread emerged.

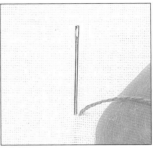

3. With your finger facing you, place the thread over your finger.

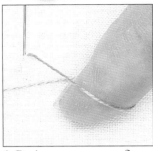

4. Begin to rotate your finger away from you. Keep the thread taut and looped around your finger.

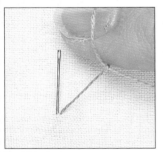

5. Continue to rotate your finger until the thread is wrapped around it.

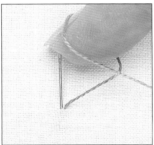

6. Keeping tension on the thread, place the tip of your finger on the end of the needle.

7. Slip the loop off your finger and onto the needle.

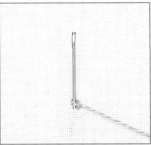

8. Pull the thread tight, slipping the loop down the needle onto the fabric.

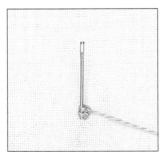

9. Work a second loop in the same manner.

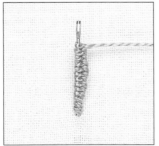

10. Continue working the required number of cast-ons in the same manner.

11. Re-thread the needle. Holding the cast-ons, begin to pull needle through.

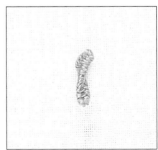

12. Pull the thread through and secure on the back of the fabric.

EYELET

Eyelets are the basis of traditional white-on-white broderie anglaise.

1. Mark a circle on the fabric. Leaving a short tail, work row of running stitches around it, leaving tiny stitches at the back.

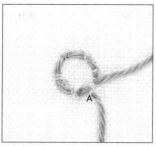

2. Work a split stitch through first stitch. Bring the thread to the front just outside the outline at A.

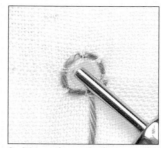

3. Trim the tail close to the fabric. Using an awl, pierce the fabric and open up the eyelet.

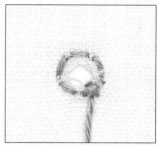

4. Take the needle down through the hole and emerge on the outer edge. Pull the thread firmly.

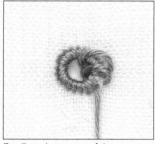

5. Continue working overcast stitches until two stitches from completing the circle. Work the final two stitches leaving them loose.

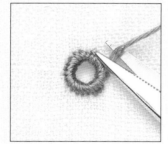

6. Take the needle through the two stitches and pull firmly. Snip the thread close to the stitching.

7. Using the awl, re-pierce the eyelet from the front and back. This helps to settle the thread and fabric.

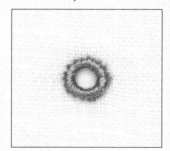

8. Finished eyelet.

EYELET — CUT

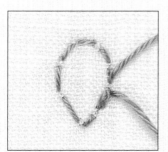

1. Work an outline of running stitch in the same manner as above.

2. Using small sharp scissors, cut the fabric into quarters at the centre of the shape.

3. Using the needle or the awl, fold each quarter of fabric under before beginning to overcast the section.

4. Complete the overcasting, trimming excess fabric on the back. Secure the thread in the same manner as above.

EYELET FILLING STITCH

Suitable as a dense filling or as isolated motifs, this pulled thread stitch is worked with pairs of back stitches. Pull each stitch firmly to open the fabric threads.

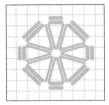

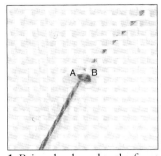

1. Bring the thread to the front at A. Take the thread to the back at B and re-emerge at A.

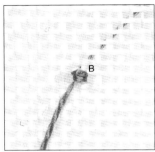

2. Take the thread to the back at B and re-emerge at A.

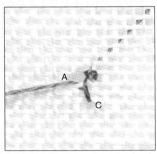

3. Take the thread to the back at C and re-emerge at A.

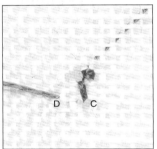

4. Take the thread to the back at C and emerge at D.

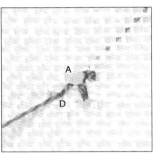

5. Take the thread to the back at A and re-emerge at D.

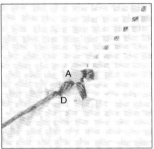

6. Take the thread to the back at A and re-emerge at D.

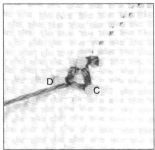

7. Take the thread to the back at C and re-emerge at D.

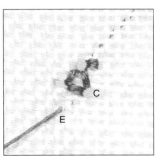

8. Take the thread to the back at C and emerge at E.

9. Continue working around the circle in this manner until the eyelet is complete.

10. If working joined eyelets, only two stitches should be worked at the point that the eyelets touch.

EYELET FLOWER

These flowers consist of an eyelet centre and granitos petals. The overcast stitches of the eyelet need to be worked very firmly, while the petals require a looser tension.

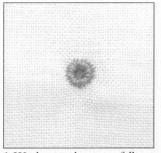  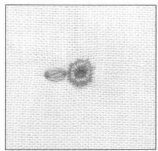 

1. Work an eyelet centre following the instructions page 73.

2. Petals. Each petal is a granitos. Work 3 stitches into the same two holes, positioning the stitches each side of the first stitch.

3. Work 13 more stitches in the same manner. The granitos should have a full, rounded look.

4. Work the remaining five petals in a similar manner. Repierce the eyelet from the back to settle the stitches.

EYELET LINE

1. Work a line of running stitches around the outline in the shape of a figure eight.

2. Using the awl, pierce each eyelet before overcasting the first edge.

Use this method when you require a trail of eyelets. When working the first pass of overcasting stitches, skip across the point where the two circles touch. Stitch this when returning with the second pass of overcasting. This prevents an unsightly lump of thread if this point is overcast twice.

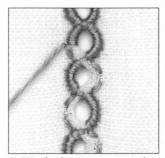 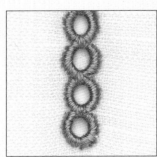

3. Work the overcast stitches following the same path as the running stitches.

4. Complete the overcasting before securing the thread in the same manner as the pierced eyelet.

FERN STITCH

This stitch is formed from three straight stitches radiating from the same central hole in the fabric. It can be worked along both curved or straight lines. Mark a line onto the fabric.

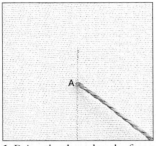

1. Bring the thread to the front at A on the line and a short distance from the end.

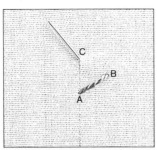

2. Take the thread to the back at B, to the right of the marked line forming a straight stitch. Pull through and emerge at C.

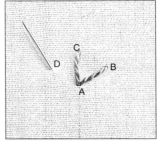

3. Pull the thread through. Take the thread to the back at A. Emerge at D, to the left of the marked line.

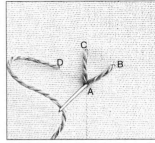

4. Pull the thread through. Take the needle to the back at A.

5. Pull the thread through.

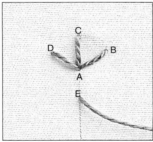

6. Bring the thread to the front at E on the line. The distance between A and E is the same as the distance between A and C.

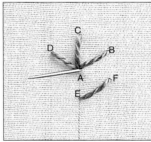

7. Take the thread to the back at F. Pull through and emerge at A through the same hole in the fabric.

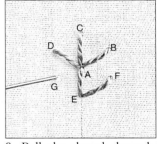

8. Pull the thread through. Take the needle to the back at E and emerge at G.

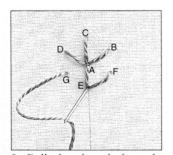

9. Pull the thread through. Take the needle to the back at E.

10. Pull the thread through to complete the second stitch.

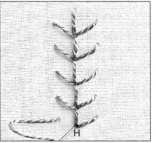

11. Continue working stitches in the same manner to the end of the line. Take the needle to the back at H and secure.

12. Completed fern stitch.

FESTOON FILLING STITCH

Worked onto even weave fabric, festoon filling creates a pattern of wavy lines worked with back stitches. Pull each stitch firmly to open the fabric threads.

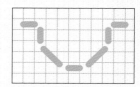

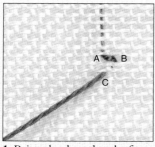

1. Bring the thread to the front at A. Take the thread to the back at B and emerge at C.

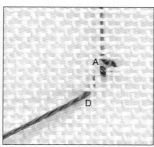

2. Take the thread to the back at A and emerge at D.

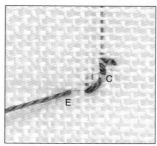

3. Take the thread to the back at C and emerge at E.

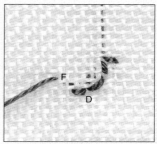

4. Take the thread to the back at D and emerge at F.

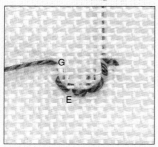

5. Take the thread to the back at E and emerge at G.

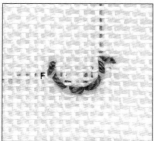

6. Take the thread to the back at F.

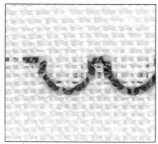

7. Repeat this sequence of stitches to the end of the row.

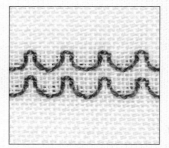

8. Work subsequent rows directly beneath the first or offset by four threads.

FINGER CHAIN

This method is used to create a row of chain stitches that are attached to the fabric only at each end.

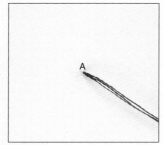

1. Secure the thread on the back of the fabric. Bring the needle to the front at A.

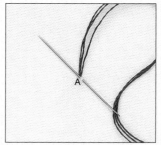

2. Take the needle to the back very close to A, leaving a loop. Re-emerge at A.

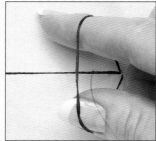

3. Leaving the needle hanging, take your fingers through the loop and grasp the thread, maintaining tension with your left hand.

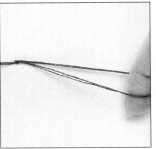  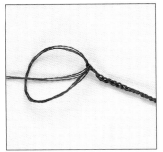 

4. Pull the thread through and allow the first loop to slide down to meet the fabric.

5. Repeat steps 3 and 4 ensuring the second chain sits firmly against the first.

6. Continue working chains as required. Take the needle through the loop and pull to secure.

7. Take the needle to the back of the fabric and secure.

FOUR SIDED STITCH

Also known as square open work stitch and four sided open work stitch. This stitch is worked from right to left.

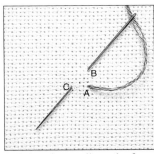 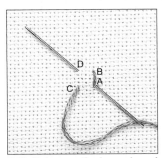

1. Bring the needle to the front at A. Take to the back at B, four threads above A. Emerge at C, four threads to the left of A.

2. Pull the needle through and insert at A. Emerge at D, four threads above C.

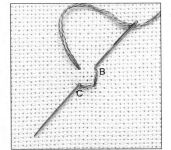 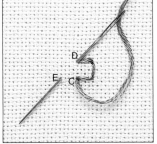 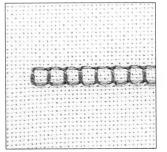 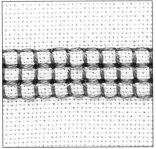

3. Insert the needle at B and emerge at C.

4. Insert the needle at D and emerge at E, four threads to the left of C.

5. Continue in this manner to the end of the row. Completed four sided stitch.

6. When working adjacent rows, use the same holes as the previous row.

FRAMED CROSS FILLING STITCH

This stitch creates an open filling of small boxes with one thread running between each box. Work this stitch in horizontal rows turning the fabric 90 degrees counter clockwise to complete the second pass of stitches.

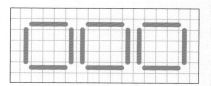

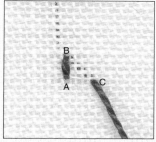

1. Bring the thread to the front at A. Take the thread to the back at B and emerge at C.

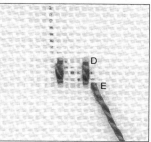

2. Take the thread to the back at D and emerge at E.

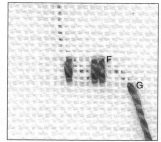

3. Take the thread to the back at F and emerge at G.

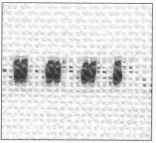

4. Continue working pairs of stitches across the row, finishing with a single stitch.

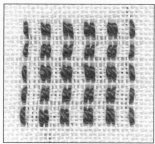

5. Continue working rows in the same manner.

6. Turn the fabric 90 degrees counter clockwise.

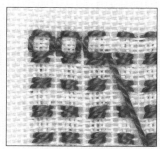

7. Work a second pass of stitches to complete the pattern.

8. Completed framed cross filling stitch.

FRENCH GLOVE STITCH

This stitch is similar to glove stitch in appearance, but is worked from right to left. It is used to join two pieces of fabric together with a decorative, visible seam.

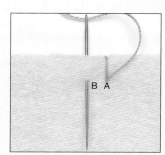

1. Bring the thread to the front at A. Take the thread over the edge and re-emerge at A.

2. Pull the thread through to form a vertical straight stitch. Take the needle over the edge and emerge at B.

french glove stitch | *continued*

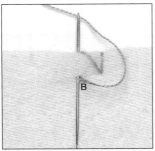 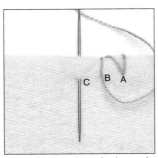 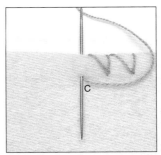 

3. Pull the thread through forming a diagonal stitch. Take the needle over the edge and re-emerge at B.

4. Pull the thread through. Take a stitch over the edge and emerge at C.

5. Pull the thread though. Work a stitch over the edge and re-emerge at C.

6. Continue in this manner for the required distance ending with a vertical stitch.

GATHERED RIBBON BLOSSOM

These flowers can be made with any number of petals. When dividing the ribbon into evenly spaced sections each section will form one petal - the more sections the more petals.

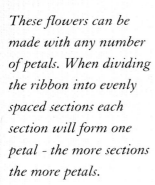 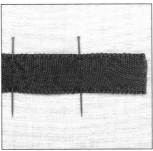 

1. Cut a piece of ribbon the required length. Mark the ribbon at evenly spaced intervals.

2. Knot a length of sewing thread. Starting approx 3mm (1/8") from one end, work tiny running stitches until almost at the opposite edge.

3. Turn the corner and work running stitch along the edge until reaching the first mark.

   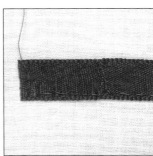

4. Turn the corner again and continue stitching to the opposite edge, ending with the needle on the back.

5. Bring the needle to the front over the edge and continue working running stitch back to the opposite edge.

6. Turn the corner and work running stitch to the second mark.

7. Continue working running stitch in the same manner to the end of the ribbon.

8. Pull up the gathers to form the petals.

9. Place the ends right sides together and stitch. Secure the thread.

10. Position the petals on the fabric and attach them with tiny stab stitches around the centre.

11. Fill the centre with a cluster of beads or knots.

GATHERED RIBBON LEAVES

Each pair of leaves in this example is made from an 8cm (3 1/4") length of ribbon.

1. Fold the ribbon in half.

2. Fold in half again so you have two loops of ribbon.

3. Work running stitch through all four layers of ribbon at the base.

4. Pull up the running stitches to gather the end.

5. Firmly wrap the thread around the base.

6. Work 2 - 3 tiny back stitches through the wraps to secure. Do not trim the excess thread.

7. The leaves are now ready to be attached to your embroidery.

8. Completed pair of leaves.

GLOVE STITCH

Traditionally used in the making of fine kid gloves, this stitch is similar in appearance to a row of zigzag stitches. It is often used to join the edges of chatelaines or boxes and makes a very pretty edge. Marking a line parallel to the edge will help to keep the stitches even.

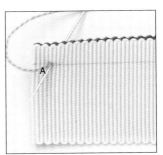

1. Bring the thread to the front at A. Take the thread over the edge and re-emerge at A.

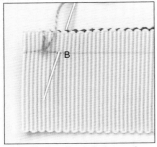

2. Pull the thread through to form a vertical straight stitch. Take the needle to the back and bring to the front at B.

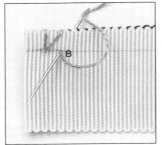

3. Pull the thread through forming a diagonal straight stitch. Take the thread over the edge and re-emerge at B.

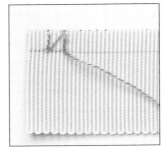

4. Pull the thread through to complete the zigzag.

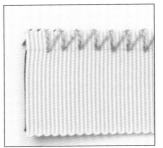

5. Continue in the same manner for the required distance, ending on a vertical stitch.

GOBELIN STITCH

Also known as diagonal Gobelin stitch, oblique Gobelin stitch and gros point, this stitch forms horizontal and vertical rows. It is often used when a wide line is required in a particular design.

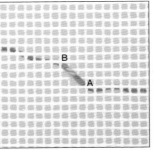

1. Bring the thread to the front at A. Take the thread to the back at B. Pull the thread through.

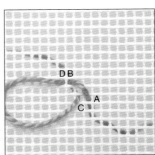

2. Emerge at C and take the thread to the back at D.

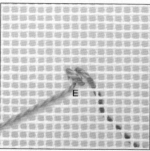

3. Pull the thread through. Bring the thread to the front at E.

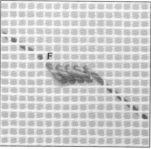

4. Continue working stitches in the same manner until reaching the first corner at F.

5. Bring the thread to the front at G.

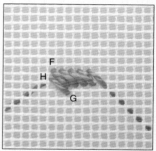

6. Take the needle to the back at H. Pull the thread through.

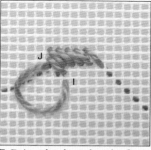

7. Bring the thread to the front at I and take it to the back at J.

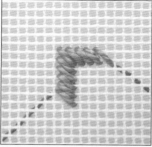

8. Pull the thread through. Continue in this manner until reaching the next corner.

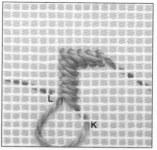

9. Bring the thread to the front at K and take to the back at L.

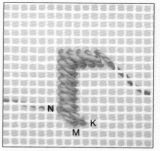

10. Pull the thread through. Bring the thread to the front at M, 1 hole to the left of K and take to the back at N. Pull the thread through.

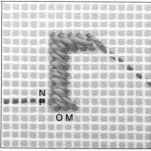

11. Bring the thread to the front at O, one hole to the left of M. Take the needle to the back at P, one hole below N. Pull the thread through.

12. Bring the thread to the front at Q. This is a shared hole at the beginning of the last stitch worked before working the corner.

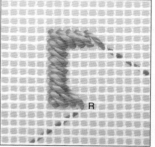

13. Take the needle to the back at R. Pull the thread through.

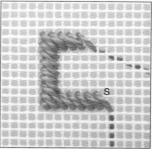

14. Bring the thread to the front at S. Continue working in the same manner until reaching the next corner.

Often mistakenly called 'tapestry', **needlepoint** is a type of counted thread embroidery worked on cotton, linen or silk canvas. The designs can be worked onto unmarked canvas using a chart, or onto printed or trammed canvas. It can be worked in a variety of threads and the most commonly used stitches are those referred to as tent stitch.

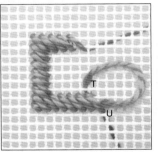 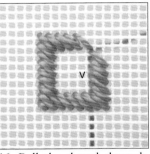 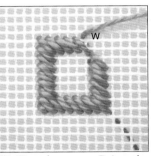 

15. Bring the thread to the front at T and take it to the back at U.

16. Pull the thread through. Bring the thread to the front at V. Continue working until reaching the next corner.

17. Fourth corner. Bring the needle to the front at W.

18. Work the last three stitches as a mirror image of the second corner.

GOBELIN FILLING STITCH

Gobelin filling is quick to work and can be used to create a border or a dense filling. Do not pull the stitches as firmly as other pulled thread stitches.

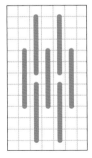 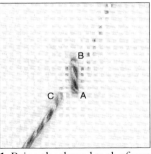

1. Bring the thread to the front at A. Take the thread to the back at B and emerge at C.

2. Continue working across the row in this manner to complete the first row.

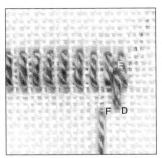  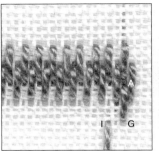 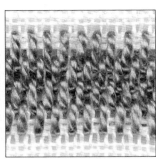

3. Bring the thread to the front at D. Take the thread to the back at E and emerge at F.

4. Continue working in this manner to complete the second row.

5. Bring the thread to the front at G. Take the thread to the back at A and emerge at I.

6. Continue working across the row in this manner to complete the third row. Work further rows if desired.

HEDEBO STITCH

Used extensively in Hedebo embroidery this stitch creates a firm edge. The edge of the fabric is cut and folded under before commencing the stitch.

1. Secure the thread and bring it up in the fold of the fabric.

2. Take a stitch through the fabric and pull through until a small loop remains.

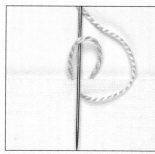

3. Take the needle, from back to front through the loop.

4. Pull the thread up until the loop sits firmly on the fabric.

5. Take a second stitch and pull through until a small loop remains.

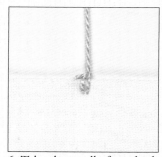

6. Take the needle from back to front through the loop and pull the thread up until the loop sits firmly on the fabric.

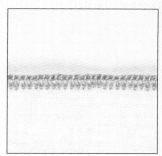

7. Continue working in this manner to the end of the line.

HERRINGBONE LADDER FILLING STITCH

This stitch is also known as laced Cretan stitch. It can be worked in a single colour or combination of colours for a pretty effect. Rule parallel lines onto the fabric to keep the lines of stitching straight. The foundation rows for this stitch are worked in Holbein stitch or, alternatively, could be worked in back stitch.

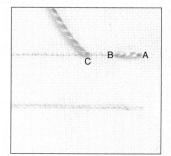

1. Bring the thread to the front at A. Take the thread to the back at B and emerge at C.

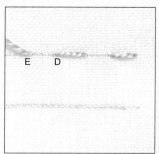

2. Take the thread to the back at D and emerge at E.

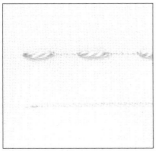

3. Continue working even running stitches across the line.

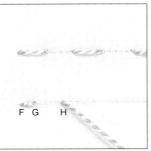

4. Bring the thread to the front at F. Take the thread to the back at G and emerge at H.

5. Continue working running stitches along the line. These stitches should be offset from the first row.

6. Beginning at the left hand end, work a second row of running stitches along both lines.

7. Bring the thread to the front at I. Slide the needle under the first stitch, ensuring that the thread is under the tip of the needle.

8. Slide the needle under the first stitch of the second row, ensuring that the thread is under the tip of the needle.

9. Slide the needle under the second foundation stitch, ensuring that the thread is under the tip of the needle.

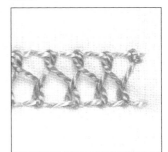

10. Continue working in this manner to the end of the row. Take the thread to the back and secure.

HONEYCOMB FILLING STITCH

Honeycomb filling is quick to work and creates an open, geometric pattern.

Pull each stitch firmly to open the fabric threads.

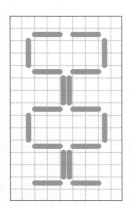

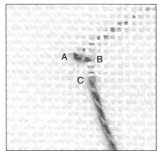

1. Bring the thread to the front at A. Take the thread to the back at B and emerge at C.

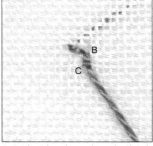

2. Take the thread to the back at B and re-emerge at C.

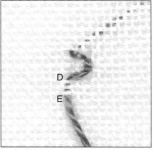

3. Take the thread to the back at D and emerge at E.

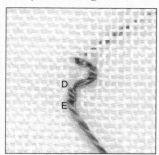

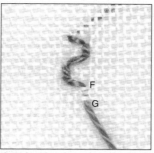

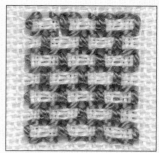

4. Take the thread to the back at D and re-emerge at E.

5. Take the thread to the back at F and emerge at G.

6. Continue working in this manner to the end of the line.

7. Work mirror image rows to fill the shape.

INTERLACED BAND STITCH

Interlaced band has a foundation of double herringbone stitch worked in a single colour. It is an intricate stitch that requires concentration. Mark temporary parallel guidelines onto the fabric. Work the interlacing with a tapestry needle.

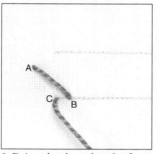

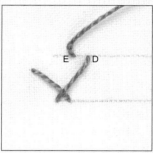

1. Bring the thread to the front at A. Take the needle to the back at B and emerge at C.

2. Take the needle to the back at D and emerge at E.

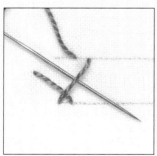

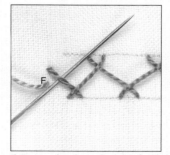

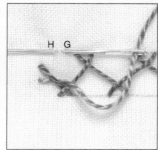

3. Slide the needle under the diagonal thread.

4. Continue working herring-bone stitch to the end of the row.

5. Bring the thread to the front at F. Slide the needle under the diagonal thread.

6. Take the needle to the back at G and emerge at H.

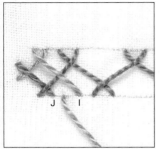

7. Take the needle to the back at I and emerge at J.

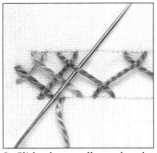

8. Slide the needle under the diagonal thread as shown.

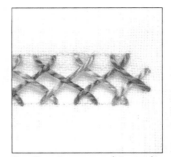

9. Continue working the second row of herringbone stitches to the end of the row.

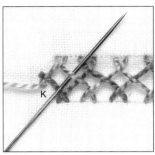

10. Bring the thread to the front at K. Slide the needle under the diagonal stitch as shown.

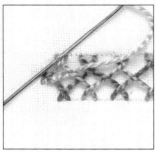

11. Slide the needle under the top of the diagonal stitch as shown.

12. Slide the needle under the working thread and the diagonal stitch as shown.

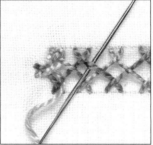

13. Slide the needle over then under the next two diagonal stitches as shown.

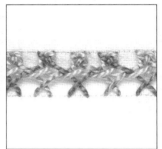

14. Repeat steps 11 - 13 to the end of the line.

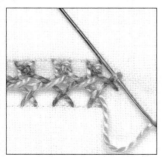

15. Take the thread around the end of the line as shown.

16. Slide the thread over the next diagonal stitch, under the working thread and under the next diagonal stitch.

17. Slide the needle under the bottom of the diagonal stitch as shown.

18. Slide the needle over, under, over, under the next four threads as shown.

Fabrics suitable for surface embroidery include: **Calico,** a firm plain, unbleached cotton fabric; **Cotton,** one of the most durable of fabrics; **Linen,** an elegant, strong and durable fabric; **Silk,** a luxurious and sensuous fabric, available in a wide variety of weights and finishes; **Furnishing fabric,** offering wonderful choices of plain colours or self-patterns, such as damask; **Felt,** a non-woven fabric that will not fray when cut; and **Wool,** ideal for baby wraps and blanketing.

interlaced band stitch | *continued*

19. Repeat steps 16 - 18 to the end of the line.

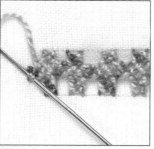

20. Take the needle around the end of the line as shown. Take the thread to the back and secure.

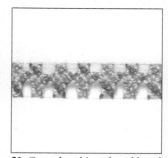

21. Completed interlaced band stitch.

INTERLACED HERRINGBONE STITCH

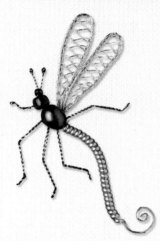

First work a foundation of back stitch along the design lines. Use a tapestry needle when working the interlacing to avoid splitting the stitches.

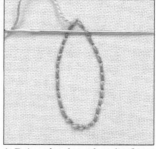

1. Bring the thread to the front under the first back stitch on the left hand side. Slide the needle from left to right under the second back stitch.

2. Pull the thread through. Slide the needle under the first back stitch from right to left.

3. Taking the needle over the lacing, slide it under the second back stitch on the left hand side. Pull the thread through.

4. Slide the needle under the first stitch. Take it over the lacing and under the third stitch on the right hand side.

5. Pull the thread through. Continue until all back stitches have been laced.

6. Take the thread to the back just under the last back stitch and secure.

ITALIAN CROSS STITCH

This lovely variation of cross stitch can be worked as a counted thread technique or as a border or filling on plain weave fabrics. Mark temporary guidelines onto the fabric if needed.

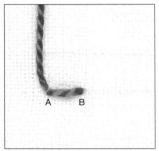

1. Bring the thread to the front at A. Take the thread to the back at B and re-emerge at A.

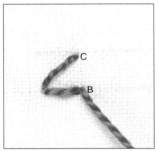

2. Take the thread to the back at C and emerge at B.

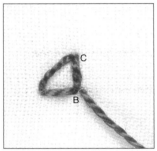

3. Take the thread to the back at C and re-emerge at B.

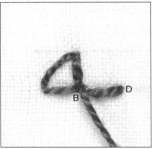

4. Take the thread to the back at D and re-emerge at B.

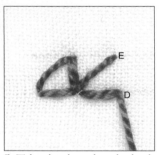

5. Take the thread to the back at E and emerge at D.

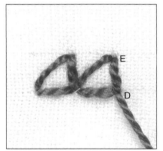

6. Take the thread to the back at E and re-emerge at D.

7. Continue working in this manner to the end of the line.

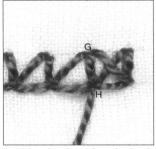

8. Take the thread to the back at G and emerge at H.

9. Take the thread to the back at I and emerge at J.

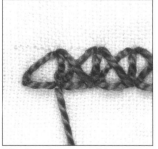

10. Continue working diagonal stitches in this manner back along the line.

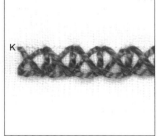

11. Take the thread to the back at K and secure.

Cross stitch, one of the oldest forms of embroidery, can be found all over the world. Many folk museums show examples of clothing decorated with cross stitch, especially from continental Europe and Asia. In the United States, the earliest known cross stitch sampler is housed at Pilgrim Hall in Plymouth, Massachusetts.

ITALIAN INSERTION STITCH

This decorative stitch can be used to join two pieces of fabric. Mark lines onto fabric or interfacing to act as a spacer.

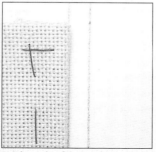

1. Place the fabric edge against one drawn line on the spacer so that the other drawn line is visible.

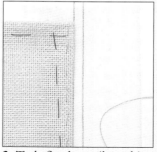

2. Tack firmly until reaching the base.

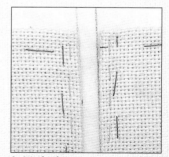

3. Tack the remaining side to the second line on the spacer interfacing.

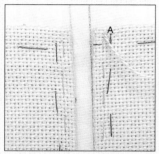

4. Bring the thread up at A, two threads in from the edge and two down from the top.

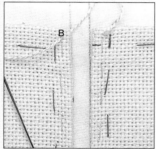

5. Bring the thread to the front at B, two threads in from the edge and two down from the top.

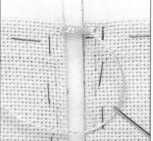

6. Repeat, working into the same holes. Work four detached blanket stitches from left to right across the loop.

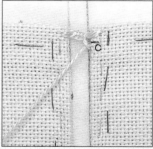

7. Work a blanket stitch on the right edge at C, two threads in from the edge and two threads down from the starting point.

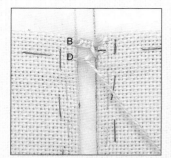

8. Work another blanket stitch on the left at D, four threads below B.

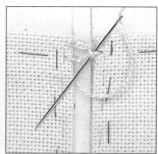

9. Work a detached blanket stitch around the centre of the blanket stitch on the right fabric edge.

10. Work three more stitches around the same stitch, working from left to right.

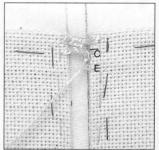

11. Work a blanket stitch on the right side at E, four threads below C.

  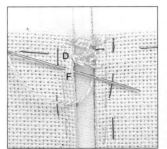 

12. Work a detached blanket stitch at the centre of the stitch on the left hand side.

13. Work three more stitches around the same stitch, working from right to left.

14. Work a blanket stitch on the left edge at F, four threads below D.

15. Continue in the same manner until reaching the base.

ITALIAN KNOTTED BORDER STITCH

This stitch creates a line of loops, each one anchored with a knot. It is almost identical to a fly stitch but is anchored with a French knot rather than a straight stitch. Alter the appearance of the stitch by changing the length and angle of the loop stitch. Mark temporary parallel guidelines onto the fabric.

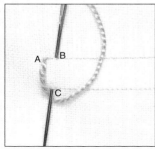 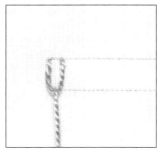 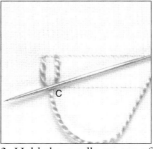 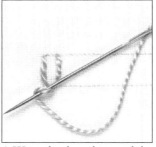

1. Bring the thread to the front at A. Take the needle to the back at B and emerge at C. Ensure that the thread is under the tip of the needle.

2. Pull the thread through until the loop sits snugly on the fabric

3. Hold the needle on top of the thread and close to C.

4. Wrap the thread around the needle as shown.

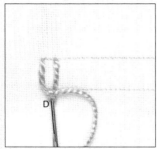 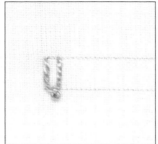 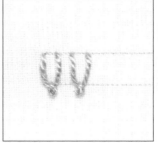 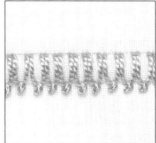

5. Insert the tip at D, outside the loop.

6. Pull the thread through to the back.

7. Work a second stitch in the same manner, close to the first.

8. Close Italian knotted border stitch.

KLOSTER BLOCKS

Kloster blocks form the basis of Hardanger embroidery. They are worked in satin stitch and consist of five parallel stitches over a grid of four by four fabric threads.

Each block is worked at a right angle to the previous one. The corners of the two blocks share the same hole in the fabric.

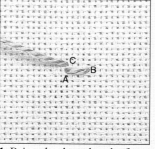

1. Bring the thread to the front at A. Take to the back at B and emerge at C.

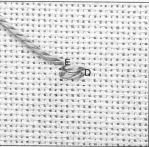

2. Take the thread to the back at D and emerge at E.

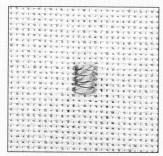

3. Continue in this manner until five stitches have been worked.

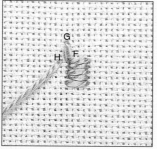

4. Bring the thread to the front at F and take it to the back at G. Emerge at H.

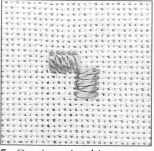

5. Continue in this manner until five stitches have been worked.

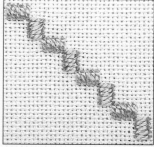

6. Continue working blocks following the chart.

KLOSTER BLOCKS — CUTTING AWAY THREAD

In preparation for needleweaving, the fabric threads are cut and removed after the relevant kloster blocks have been completed. Do not remove all the threads at once as this may destabilise the fabric. Work approximately 5cm (2") at a time.

1. Carefully cut the threads to the left of the kloster block.

2. In a similar manner, cut the fabric threads of the kloster block directly opposite.

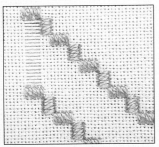

3. Remove the fabric threads cut in steps 1 and 2.

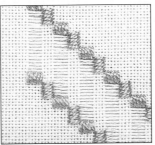

4. Repeat in the same manner to remove all the required vertical threads.

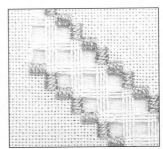

5. Remove all relevant horizontal threads the same manner.

KLOSTER BLOCKS — NEEDLEWOVEN

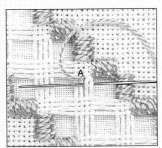

1. Bring the thread to the front at A. Take the needle around two threads on the right. Come up through the centre.

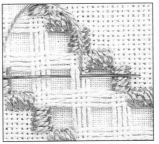

2. Tighten the stitch. Take the needle around the two threads on the left and come up through the centre.

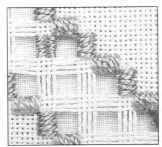

3. Tighten the stitch. Continue in this manner until the bar is filled.

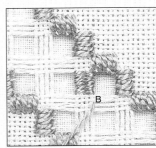

4. Carry the thread behind the fabric and bring to the front at B to begin the next bar.

KNOTTED BRAID

Knotted braid can be worked onto a fabric or as a detached cord.

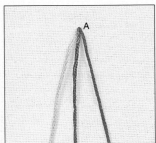

1. Bring the threads to the front at A.

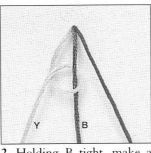

2. Holding B tight, make a loop with Y as shown.

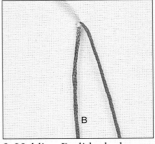

3. Holding B, slide the loop to the top and tighten the knot.

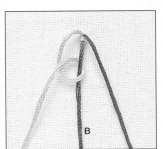

4. Using the same two threads, knot Y onto B in the same manner.

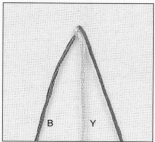

5. Tighten the knot so that B is now on the left of Y. Keep an even tension as you work.

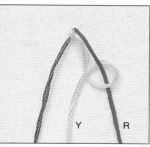

6. Following step 2, and using Y, form a loop over R as shown.

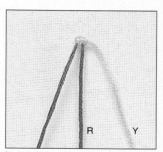

7. Tighten the loop and using the same two threads knot Y onto R. R is now in the centre, Y to the right.

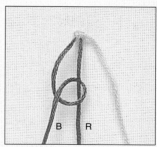

8. Following step 2 and using B, form a loop over R, as shown.

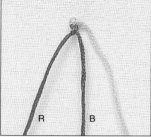

9. Tighten the loop and repeat the knot as before. R is now to the left of B.

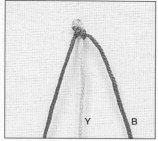

10. Following step 2, use B to form a loop over Y. Tighten and repeat. Y is now in the centre and B is to the right.

11. Continue knotting the braid, repeating the pattern formed in steps 2 - 10.

12. When the braid is the required length, tie a knot to secure. Trim the ends.

KNOTTED LOOP STITCH

Also known as loop stitch and centipede stitch, knotted loop forms a braided line and can be worked as a surface or counted thread stitch.

Mark temporary parallel guidelines onto the fabric. Vary the density of the line by spacing the stitches apart or close together.

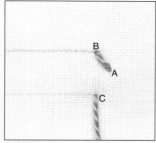

1. Bring the thread to the front at A. Take the thread to the back at B and emerge at C.

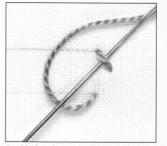

2. Slide the needle under the diagonal stitch, ensuring the thead is under the tip of the needle.

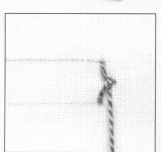

3. Pull the thread through.

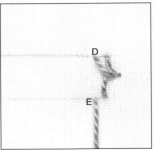 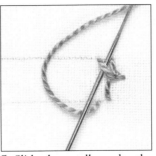  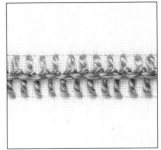

4. Take the thread to the back at D and emerge at E.

5. Slide the needle under the diagonal stitch, ensuring that the thread is under the tip of the needle.

6. Pull the thread through.

7. Continue working in this manner to the end of the line.

KNOTTED PEARL STITCH

This decorative stitch makes a perfect edging or attractive border.

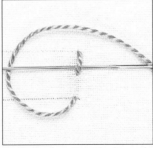 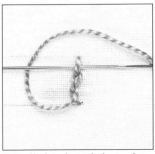

1. Bring the needle to the front at A. Take a stitch from B to C.

2. Pull the thread through. Slide the needle under the first stitch, ensuring the thread is under the tip of the needle.

3. Pull the thread through to form a knot. Slide the needle under the first stitch, ensuring the thread is under the tip of the needle.

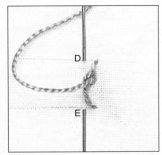   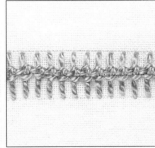

4. Pull the thread through. Insert the needle at D and emerge at E.

5. Pull the yarn through. Slide the needle under the previous stitch, ensuring the thread is under the tip of the needle.

6. Pull the thread through and repeat for a second knot.

7. Continue in this manner for the required length.

KNOTTED SHEAF STITCH

This attractive stitch is formed by parallel vertical stitches tied at the centre with a coral knot.
Work the stitches from right to left.

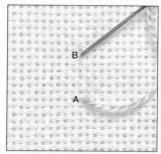 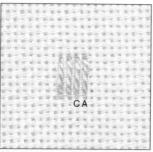 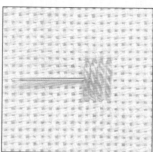 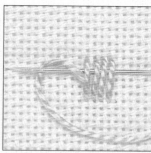

1. Bring the thread to the front at A. Take it to the back at B, six threads above A.

2. Emerge at C, one thread to the left of A. Work three straight stitches parallel to the first.

3. Bring the thread to the front under the centre of the four stitches, keeping all the stitches to the right of the needle.

4. Pull through. Slide the needle from right to left under the stitches. Wrap the thread around the tip of the needle.

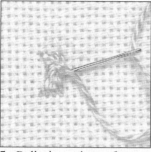  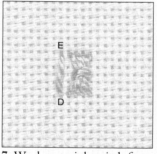 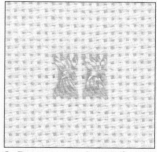

5. Pull through to form a knot. Take the needle to the back under the centre.

6. Pull the thread through. Completed first stitch.

7. Work a straight stitch from D to E, one thread to the left of the last stitch.

8. Repeat steps 2 to 6 for the second stitch.

LADDER STITCH I

Ladder stitch is used to close the opening of seams and for turning under a raw seam on appliqué work. It is worked from the right side of the fabric.

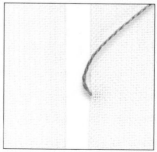 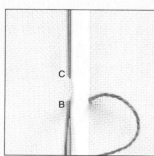

1. Bring the thread to the front on the seam line at the base of the opening (A).

2. Slide the needle through the folded edge from B to C.

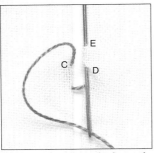

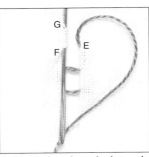

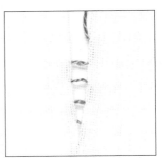

3. Pull the thread through. Slide the needle through the first folded edge from D, opposite C, to E.

4. Pull the thread through. Slide the needle through the folded edge from F, opposite E, to G.

5. Pull the thread firmly to tighten the stitches.

6. Continue working in this manner along the seamline.

7. Pull the stitches firmly every 3 - 4 stitches to close the opening.

8. Continue working in this manner to the end of the line. End off securely.

Preparing fabric for embroidery

Pre-wash fabrics according to the specified care instructions to test for shrinkage and colourfastness.

To prevent the raw edges from fraying while stitching, neaten all edges with a machine zigzag or overlock stitch.

Avoid using tape to seal the edges as the glue may permanently discolour the fabric and will attract dirt.

Ensure you allow enough fabric around the design for the intended purpose of the finished piece.

LADDER STITCH 2

This stitch can be used to form a dense border or a filling for long, narrow shapes and is suitable as a surface or counted thread stitch. Mark parallel lines onto the fabric.

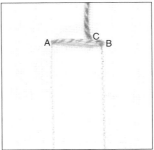

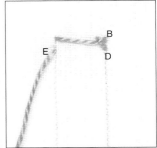

1. Bring the thread to the front at A. Take the thread to the back at B and emerge at C.

2. Take the thread to the back at D, directly below B, and emerge at E.

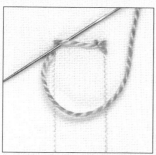

3. Slide the needle under the horizontal stitch as shown.

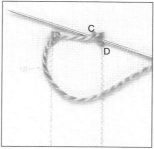

4. Slide the needle through the right hand end, above D and below C as shown.

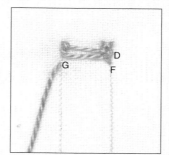

5. Take the needle to the back at F, directly below D, and emerge at G.

6. Slide the needle, from right to left, behind the thread loop as shown.

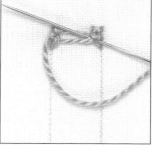

7. Slide the needle, from right to left, behind the thread loop as shown.

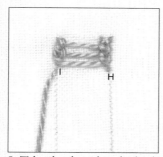

8. Take the thread to the back at H and emerge at I.

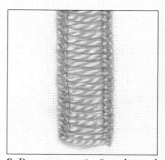

9. Repeat steps 6 - 8 to the end of the row.

LEAF STITCH

This open, light stitch can be used as a border but is also ideal for filling round, oval and leaf shapes.

It forms a solid central line with angled arms. Begin at the base of the shape and work upwards.

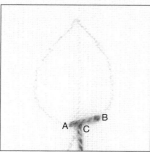

1. Bring the thread to the front at A. Take it to the back at B and emerge at C.

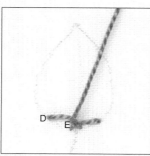

2. Take the thread to the back at D and emerge at E.

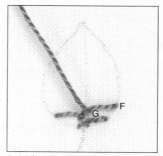

3. Take the thread to the back at F and emerge at G.

4. Continue working in this manner to the end of the shape.

LEVIATHAN DOUBLE STITCH VARIATION

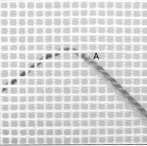

1. Bring the thread to the front at A. This is the hole at the top left hand corner of the square that the stitch will cover.

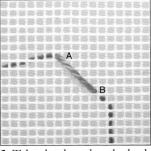

2. Take the thread to the back at B.

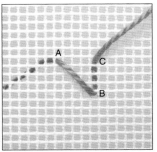

3. Emerge at C.

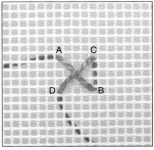

4. Take the thread to the back at D.

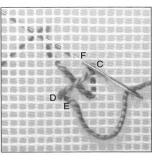

5. Emerge at E. Take the thread to the back at F.

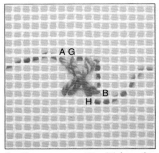

6. Emerge at G. Take the thread to the back at H.

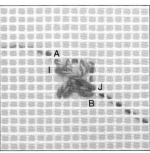

7. Emerge at I. Take the thread to the back at J.

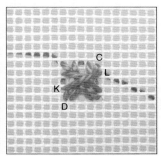

8. Emerge at K. Take the thread to the back at L.

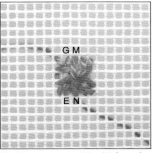

9. Emerge at M. Take the thread to the back at N.

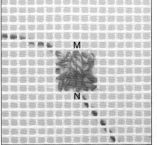

10. Work a second stitch from M to N. Ensure they lie side by side.

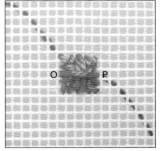

11. Emerge at O. Take the thread to the back at P.

During the Middle Ages, **linen and hempen cloth** were used as a ground for needlepoint. Linen was produced from the flax plant and hempen cloth was a product of the cannabis plant, along with rope, oil, sailcloth and tents. While much has been made of linen, it appears to have been rivalled by hemp.

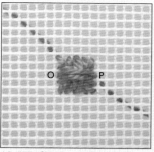

12. Work a second stitch from O to P ensuring they lie side by side.

13. Bring the thread to the front at C to begin the second stitch.

14. Work this stitch in the same manner.

MADEIRA PIN STITCH

As this stitch is worked, tiny holes are created when the horizontal threads in the fabric are pulled together.

It is important to maintain a firm, even tension on the thread throughout. A finger shield is recommended for protecting the finger of your left hand as the needle passes through to the back of the fabric.

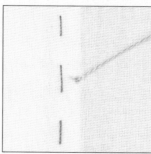
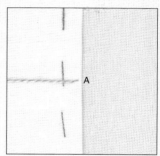

1. Work a small back stitch on the back to secure the thread, ensuring it does not show on the front.

2. Bring the needle and thread to the front at A.

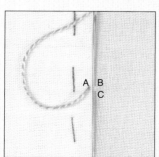
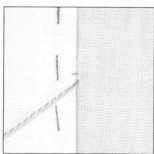
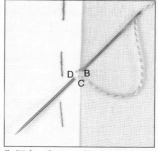
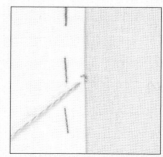

3. Take the needle from B to C on the cream fabric.

4. Pull the thread through.

5. Take the needle to the back at B and emerge at D.

6. Pull the thread through firmly.

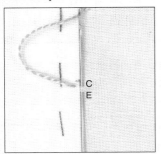

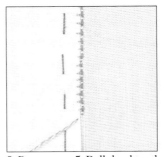

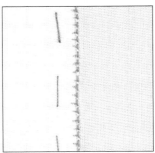

7. Take the needle to the back at C and emerge at E.

8. Pull the thread through.

9. Repeat step 5. Pull the thread through firmly. Continue working stitches in this manner.

10. To end off, take the thread to the back and secure.

MOUNTMELLICK STITCH

This stitch is synonomous with Mountmellick embroidery, a form of coarse whitework that was popular in the 19th century. Mark a line onto the fabric.

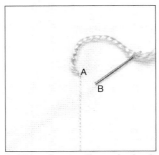

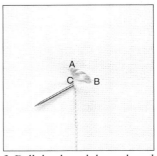

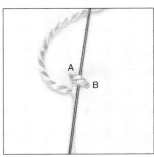

1. Bring the thread to the front at A, at the top of the line.

2. Take the needle to the back at B.

3. Pull the thread through and emerge at C.

4. Pull the thread through. Slide the needle under the stitch.

5. Pull the thread through. Loop the thread to the left, and take the needle to the back at A.

6. Pull the thread through, leaving a loop on the front.

7. Bring the needle to the front at C. Ensure it is inside the loop.

8. Pull the thread through until the loop lies snugly against the emerging thread.

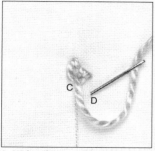

9. Take the needle to the back at D.

10. Pull the thread through and emerge at E.

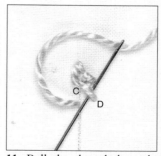

11. Pull the thread through. Slide the needle under the stitch in the same manner as before.

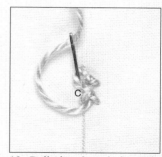

12. Pull the thread through. Loop the thread to the left and take the needle to the back at C.

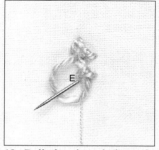

13. Pull the thread through, leaving a loop. Bring the needle to the front at E inside the loop.

14. Pull the thread through until the loop lies snugly against the emerging thread.

15. Continue working in the same manner. After the last stitch, take the needle to the back just over the last loop.

16. Pull the thread through and secure on the back.

MOSAIC DIAMOND FILLING STITCH

Mosaic diamond filling is worked onto even weave fabric with easily counted threads but the stitches should not be pulled firmly as in other pulled fabric stitches. It forms a dense covering and is quick to work.

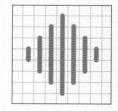

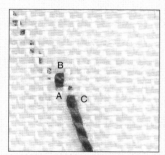

1. Bring the thread to the front at A. Take the thread to the back at B and emerge at C.

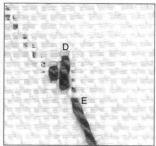

2. Take the thread to the back at D and emerge at E.

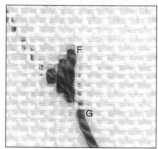

3. Take the thread to the back at F and emerge at G.

4. Take the thread to the back at H and emerge at I.

5. Work three more stitches to create a diamond.

6. Continue working in this manner across the row.

7. Closely spaced diamonds.

8. Widely spaced diamonds.

MOSAIC FILLING STITCH

This stitch creates a heavy, blocked surface with a contrasting cross stitch at the centre of each motif. It can be used as a filling stitch or as single, scattered motifs. Pull each stitch firmly to open the fabric threads.

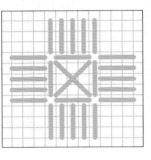

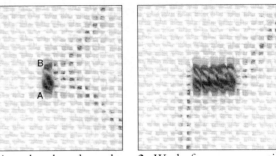

1. Bring the thread to the front at A. Take the thread to the back at B.

2. Work four more vertical straight stitches, each one a thread apart.

3. Work five horizontal straight stitches, beginning at the base of the last stitch of the vertical row.

4. Work two more sets of five stitches to complete the square. The first and last stitch of each row should share holes with the adjoining row.

5. Bring the thread to the front at C. Take the thread to the back at D and emerge at E.

6. Take the thread to the back at C and emerge at F.

mosaic filling stitch | *continued*

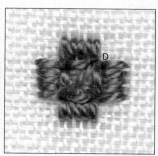

7. Take the thread to the back at D and emerge at E.

8. Take the thread to the back at F and emerge at C.

9. Take the thread to the back at F and emerge at E.

10. Take the thread to the back at D to complete the stitch.

MOSS STITCH

These isolated stitches create an interesting texture when scattered within a shape.

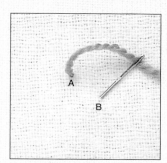

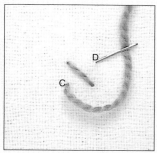

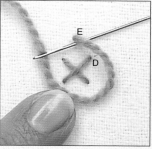

1. Bring the thread to the front at A. Take the needle to the back at B.

2. Pull the thread through to form a diagonal straight stitch. Bring the needle to the front at C. Pull the thread through and take the needle to the back at D.

3. Pull the thread through to form a cross stitch. Bring the thread to the front at E.

4. Form a loop in the thread in the manner shown.

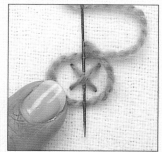

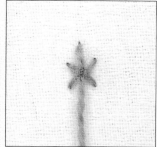

5. Holding the loop in place, slide the needle from top to bottom behind the centre of the cross.

6. Ensure the loop is under the tip of the needle. Pull the thread through until a small knot lies at the centre of the cross.

7. Take the needle to the back at F.

8. Pull the thread through and end off on the back of the fabric.

NEW ENGLAND LAID STITCH

A characteristic stitch of Deerfield embroidery, this filling stitch is very similar to Roumanian couching but with a longer centre couching stitch. Worked closely together, it could be mistaken for long and short stitch, which was not used in traditional Deerfield embroidery.

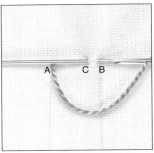

1. Bring the thread to the front at A. Keeping the thread below, take the needle to the back at B and emerge at C.

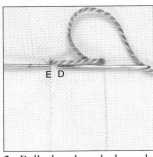

2. Pull the thread through. Keeping the thread above, take the needle from D to E, parallel to the previous stitch.

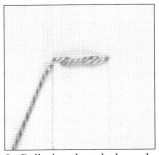

3. Pull the thread through, creating a long couching stitch.

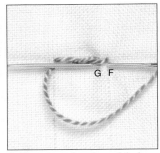

4. Keeping the thread below, take the needle from F to G, just below the first stitch.

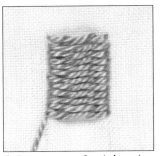

5. Repeat steps 2 - 4, keeping the stitches very close together.

OBLIQUE FILLING STITCH

Oblique filling is a pulled thread stitch that creates an open lattice intersected with holes. Pull each stitch as firmly as possible to open the fabric threads.

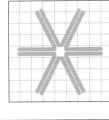

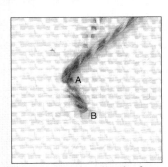

1. Bring the thread to the front at A. Take the thread to the back at B and re-emerge at A.

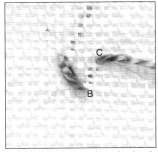

2. Take the thread to the back at B and emerge at C.

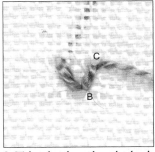

3. Take the thread to the back at B and re-emerge at C.

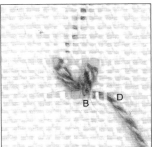

4. Take the thread to the back at B and emerge at D.

oblique filling stitch | *continued*

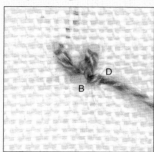 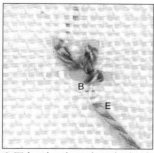  

5. Take the thread to the back at B and re-emerge at D.

6. Take the thread to the back at B and emerge at E.

7. Continue working in a circle ensuring that there is a double stitch to each point.

8. Continue working motifs to fill the required shape.

PEARL STITCH

Similar to coral stitch, this stitch creates a pebbled line that varies in appearance according to the closeness of the stitches. Use a heavy round thread such as cotton perlé for the best effect. Mark a guideline onto the fabric.

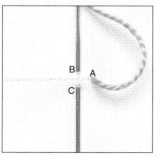 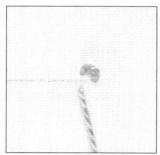  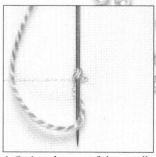

1. Bring thread to the front at A. Take the thread to the back at B and emerge at C.

2. Pull the thread through leaving a small loop.

3. Slide the needle, from left to right, under the loop.

4. Swing the top of the needle to the right and slide the tip under the working thread.

  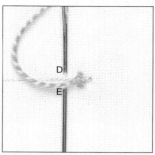 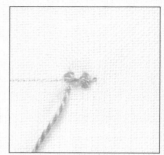

5. Pull the thread through.

6. Tighten the thread to form a knot.

7. Take the needle to the back at D and emerge at E.

8. Pull the thread through, leaving a small loop.

pearl stitch | *continued*

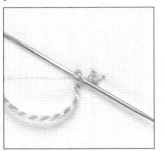

9. Slide the needle, from left to right, under the loop.

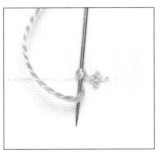

10. Swing the top of the needle to the right and slide the tip under the working thread.

11. Pull the thread through. Tighten the thread to form a knot.

12. Continue working in this manner to the end of the row.

PEKINESE STITCH

Also known as Chinese stitch, blind stitch and forbidden stitch. Pekinese stitch can be worked as a single line or a filling stitch. Maintain an even stitch tension to ensure that all loops are the same size.

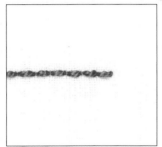

1. Work a foundation row of evenly spaced back stitches.

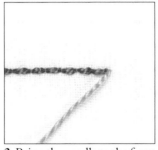

2. Bring the needle to the front at the end of the row.

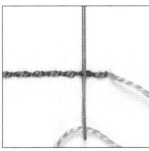

3. Slide the needle, from bottom to top, under the second stitch.

4. Pull the thread through. Slide the needle, from top to bottom, under the first stitch and over the working thread.

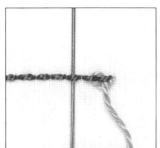

5. Slide the needle, from bottom to top, under the third stitch.

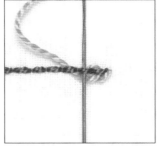

6. Slide the needle, from top to bottom, under the second stitch and over the working thread.

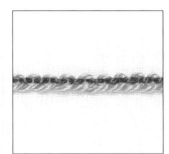

7. Continue working in this manner to the end of the row.

PLAITED BRAID STITCH

A favourite of Elizabethan embroiderers, this stitch can be difficult to work unless a heavy, firm thread is used. In surviving examples of Elizabethan embroidery, it was often worked with stiff metal thread. This is a complex stitch and requires practice to perfect but is well worth the effort.

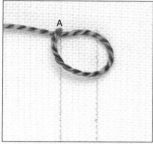

1. Bring the thread to the front at A. Form a thread loop, as shown.

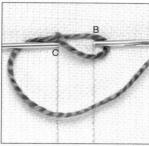

2. Take the thread to the back at B and emerge at C, ensuring that the working thread is under the tip of the needle.

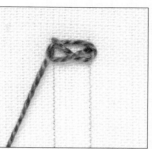

3. Pull the thrtead through.

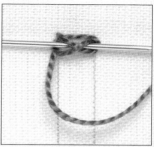

4. Slide the needle under the centre threads as shown.

5. Take the needle to the back at D and emerge at E.

6. Slide the needle from right to left under the central threads as shown.

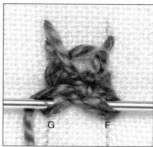

7. Form a loop. Take the needle to the back at F and emerge at G.

8. Continue working steps 6 - 7 to the end of the row.

PLAITED EDGE STITCH

This lovely stitch is similar in appearance to blanket stitch and has a pretty plaited edge. It is very hard wearing making it suitable for the hemmed edges of household linens.
Any type of embroidery thread is suitable.

1. Bring the thread through the folded edge of the hem.

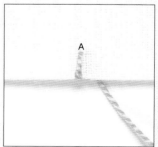

2. Take the thread to the back at A, forming a straight stitch.

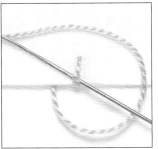

3. Slide the needle, from left to right, under the straight stitch.

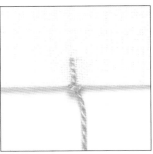

4. With the working thread under the tip of the needle, pull the thread through.

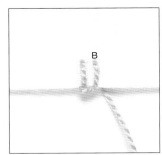

5. Take the thread to the back at B, forming a straight stitch.

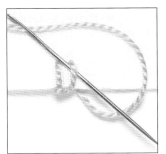

6. Slide the needle, from left to right, under the straight stitch.

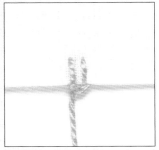

7. With the working thread under the tip of the needle, pull the thread through.

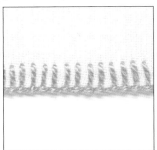

8. Continue working in this manner to the end of the line.

Making pompoms

Discs, especially for making pompoms, can be purchased from specialist knitting or sewing shops.

The larger the hole in your discs, the fuller your pompom will be. However, if your hole is too large, your pompom will end up oval shaped.

POMPOM

From the French 'pompon', a pompom is a ball of thread, that can be used to ornament embroidery and knitting. This example is formed by wrapping wool around a doughnut shaped piece of cardboard.

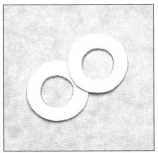

1. Cut two circles of card the required size.

2. Place the pieces of card together. Using a long length of wool and a chenille needle, take it through the hole and knot it at the edge.

3. Take the wool through the hole again and around the outer edge.

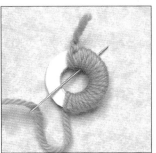

4. Always working in the same direction, continue taking the wool through the hole so it wraps around the cardboard.

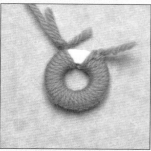

5. To join in a new piece of wool, knot the new length to the end of the old piece, positioning the knot at the outer edge.

6. Continue wrapping the wool around the cardboard in the same manner until the hole is very firmly packed.

7. Place small sharp scissors between the two pieces of card at the outer edge and cut through the wool.

8. Cut a short length of wool. Take it between the two pieces of card so it encircles the cut pieces of wool at the centre. Tie in a firm secure knot.

9. Carefully cut through each piece of cardboard and gently remove them.

10. Fluff out the cut strands with your fingers to make a ball shape.

11. Carefully trim away any knots or uneven pieces of wool.

12. Completed pompom.

PUNCH STITCH

A pulled thread technique, punch stitch produces an even grid with holes at each intersection. Pull each stitch firmly to open the fabric threads.

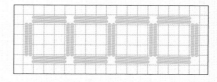

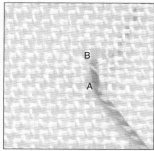

1. Bring the thread to the front at A. Take the thread to the back at B and re-emerge at A.

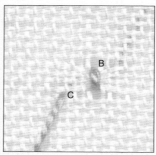

2. Take the thread to the back at B and emerge at C

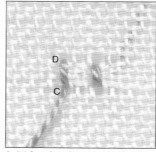

3. Take the thread to the back at D and re-emerge at C.

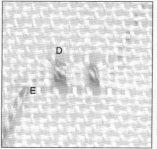

4. Take the thread to the back at D and emerge at E.

 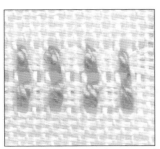 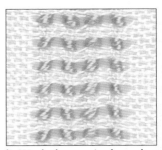 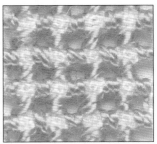

5. Continue working in this manner to the end of the row.

6. Work a second row of stitches from left to right.

7. Work the required number of rows. Turn the work 90 degrees counter clockwise.

8. Repeat the rows of double stitches in the same manner to complete the squares.

RAISED BLANKET STITCH

Similar to raised stem stitch, raised blanket produces a more open filling over the foundation bars. It is worked from top to bottom for each row. Mark parallel guidelines onto the fabric.

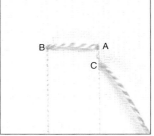 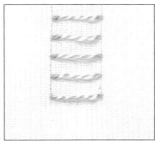 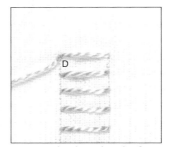 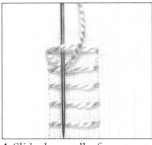

1. Bring the thread to the front at A. Take the thread to the back at B and emerge at C.

2. Continue working small horizontal stitches in this manner to the end of the shape.

3. Bring the thread to the front at D, below B.

4. Slide the needle, from top to bottom, under the first foundation stitch. Ensure that the working thread is under the tip of the needle.

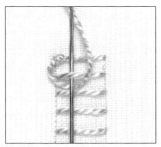 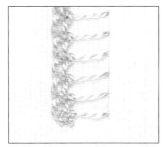 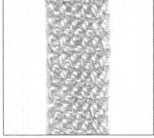

5. Slide the needle, from top to bottom, under the second foundation stitch. Ensure that the working thread is under the tip of the needle.

6. Continue working in this manner to the end of the row. Take the thread to the back over the last loop and secure. Return to the top and work a second row.

7. Continue working rows from the top until the foundation bars are full.

RAISED CHAIN BAND

This is a lovely stitch for borders and stems and can be worked in a single colour or a combination. It is worked from the top of the shape down towards the base.

Mark temporary parallel guidelines onto the fabric.

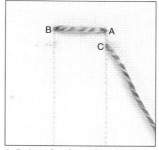

1. Bring the thread to the front at A. Take the thread to the back at B and emerge at C.

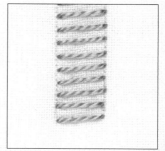

2. Continue working small horizontal stitches in this manner to the end of the shape.

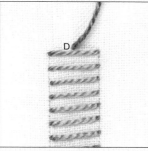

3. Bring the second thread to the front at D.

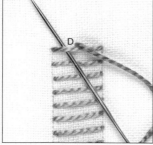

4. Take the thread over the first foundation stitch. Slide the needle, from bottom to top, under this stitch, emerging to the left of D.

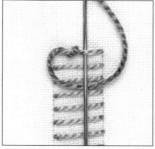

5. Slide the needle, from top to bottom, under the foundation stitch, ensuring the thread is under the tip of the needle.

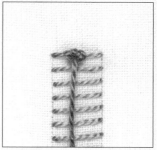

6. Pull the thread through, forming a loop.

7. Slide the needle, from bottom to top, under the second foundation stitch, emerging on the left hand side.

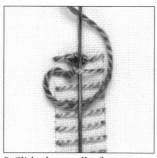

8. Slide the needle, from top to bottom, under the second foundation stitch, ensuring the thread is under the tip of the needle.

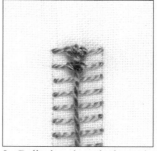

9. Pull the thread through, forming a loop.

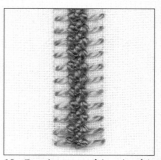

10. Continue working in this manner to the end of the row. Take the thread to the back and secure.

RAISED CHAIN BAND VARIATION

This variation of raised chain creates a smooth surface that resembles knitted stocking stitch. The foundation stitches are completely covered. Mark parallel guidelines onto the fabric.

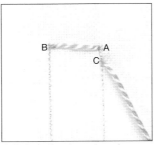

1. Bring the thread to the surface at A. Take the thread to the back at B and emerge at C.

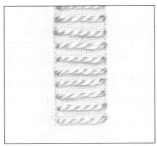

2. Continue working small horizontal stitches in this manner to the end of the shape.

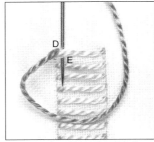

3. Bring the thread to the front at D. Take the needle to the back at D and emerge at E, under the first foundation stitch. Do not pull the thread through.

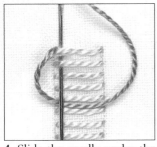

4. Slide the needle under the second foundation stitch. Ensure the thread is under the tip of the needle.

5. Pull the thread through.

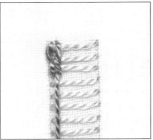

6. Slide the needle under the second and third foundation stitches. With the thread under the tip of the needle pull through.

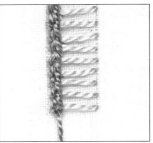

7. Continue working chain over the bars ensuring that each chain uses one used and one new foundation bar.

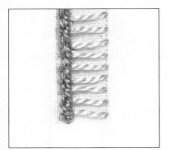

8. Take the thread to the back over the loop of the last stitch and secure.

9. Work subsequent rows in the same manner.

RAISED CLOSE HERRINGBONE STITCH

This lovely stitch is perfect for working raised leaves. It is a 'self-padding' stitch and is quick and easy to work. The stitch will slant towards the end where the straight stitch has been worked.

Use a tapestry needle to avoid catching threads.

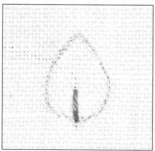

1. Work a straight stitch from the base of the leaf to a point 1/3 along the length.

2. Bring the thread to the front at the tip of the leaf.

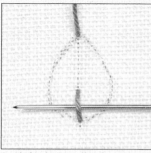

3. Slide the needle, from right to left, under the straight stitch.

4. Take the thread to the back at the tip to the right of the first stitch.

5. Emerging at A, work a second stitch in the same manner, just below the first stitch.

6. Continue working, moving down the sides of the shape until it is full. Finish with a stitch on the right hand side.

RAISED KNOT STITCH

Also known as square boss, this stitch has the appearance of a cross worked through a circle and is useful as an isolated stitch but can also be worked as a border.

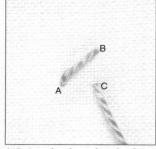

1. Bring the thread to the front at A, Take the thread to the back at B and emerge at C.

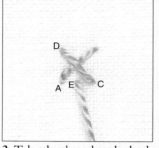

2. Take the thread to the back at D and emerge at E, between A and C.

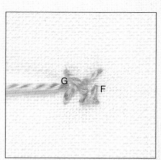

3. Take the thread to the back at F and emerge at G.

 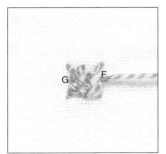  

4. Take the thread to the back at E and emerge at H.

5. Take the thread to the back at G and emerge at F.

6. Take the thread to the back at H and secure.

RAY STITCH

This is also known as fan stitch. It is usually worked over three vertical and three horizontal fabric threads.

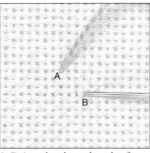 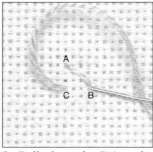 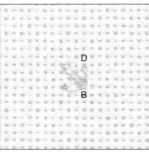

1. Bring the thread to the front at A. Take the needle to the back at B.

2. Pull through. Bring the thread to the front at C. Take the needle to the back at B.

3. Pull through. Bring the thread to the front at D and take it to the back at B.

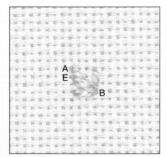 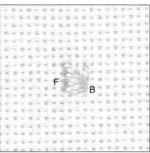 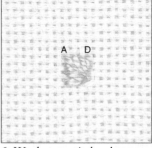 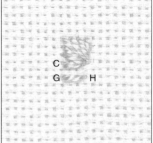

4. Bring the thread to the front at E. Take it to the back at B.

5. Take a stitch from F to B in the same manner.

6. Work two stitches between A and D in the same manner.

7. Bring the thread to the front at G. Work a stitch from G to H.

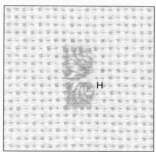

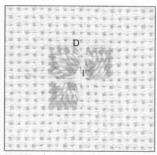

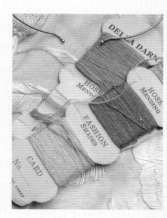

8. Complete the ray stitch, working all six stitches into the same hole at H.

9. Work a third ray stitch, placing the first stitch two threads to the right of D taking all stitches to the back at I.

10. Repeat for the last ray stitch, spacing it two fabric threads to the right and below the previous stitches.

RENAISSANCE STITCH

This versatile stitch can be used as a border, filling or as an isolated stitch in varying sizes.

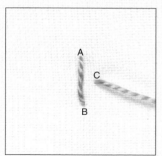

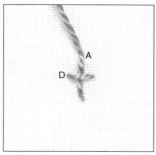

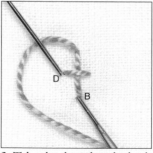

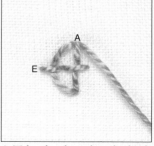

1. Bring the thread to the front at A. Take the thread to the back at B and emerge at C.

2. Take the thread to the back at D and emerge at A.

3. Take the thread to the back at B and emerge at D, ensuring that the thread is under the tip of the needle.

4. Take the thread to the back at E and emerge at A.

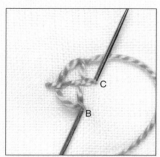

5. Take the thread to the back at B and emerge at C, ensuring that the thread is under the tip of the needle.

6. Take the thread to the back at F and secure.

The word '**renaissance**' means rebirth and refers to a period in history between 1350AD to 1600AD. It began in Italy and quickly spread to other parts of Europe, focusing on the potential of man during life rather than relating the meaning of life on Earth to the afterlife as had been the case during the Middle ages.

The Renaissance was a time of great intellectual and artistic development and was inspired by the renewed study of classical literature and art. Some of histories greatest artists, such as Leonardo da Vinci and Michelangelo lived during this time.

RHODES STITCH

Rhodes stitch was invented by British needlework designer, Mary Rhodes. The size of the stitch can vary, covering anything from three to twenty-four horizontal and vertical canvas threads. Here the stitches are worked over four horizontal and four vertical canvas threads (five holes). Begin each Rhodes stitch with a stitch at the same angle so every square looks the same.

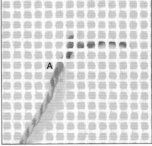

1. Bring the thread to the front at A. This is one hole below the top left hand corner of the square to be covered.

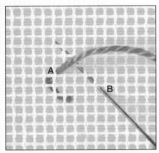

2. Take the needle to the back at B.

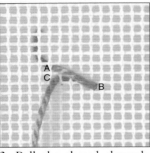

3. Pull the thread through. Emerge at C, directly below A.

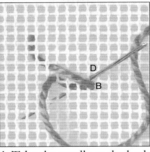

4. Take the needle to the back at D, directly above B.

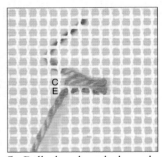

5. Pull the thread through. Emerge at E, directly below C.

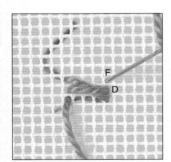

6. Take the needle to the back at F, directly above D.

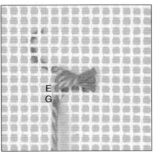

7. Pull the thread through. Emerge at G, directly below E.

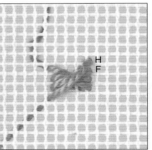

8. Take the needle to the back at H, directly above F. Pull the thread through.

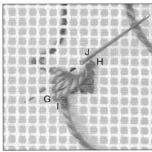

9. Emerge at I, one hole to the right of G. Take the needle to the back at J, one hole to the left of H.

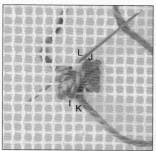 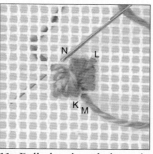 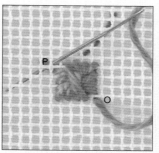 

10. Pull the thread through. Emerge at K, one hole to the right of I. Take the needle to the back at L, one hole to the left of J.

11. Pull the thread through. Emerge at M, one hole to the right of K. Take the needle to the back at N.

12. Pull the thread through. Emerge at O in the lower right hand corner. Take the needle to the back at P, in the upper left hand corner.

13. Pull the thread through.

RIDGE FILLING STITCH

A variation of cross stitch, ridge filling creates diagonal lines of interlocking upright crosses on even weave fabric. The diagonal fabric ridges are created by pulling each stitch as firmly as possible.

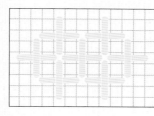 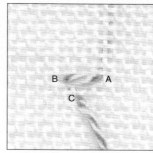 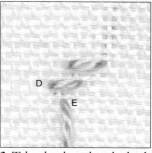

1. Bring the thread to the front at A. Take the thread to the back at B and emerge at C.

2. Take the thread to the back at D and emerge at E.

  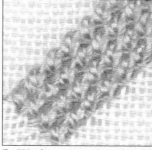 

3. Continue working diagonally stepped stitches to the end of the row.

4. Work back up the row with vertical stitches, sharing holes from the first row.

5. Work a second and subsequent rows in the same manner, sharing holes with previous rows.

RINGED BACK FILLING STITCH

This stitch creates rows of circles and is worked in two overlapping rows of waves. Pull each stitch firmly to open the fabric threads.

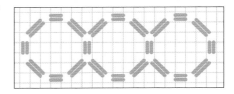

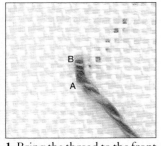

1. Bring the thread to the front at A. Take the thread to the back at B and re-emerge at A.

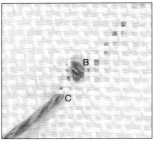

2. Take the thread to the back at B and emerge at C.

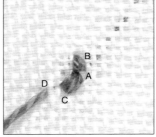

3. Work two stitches between C and A, emerging at D after the second stitch.

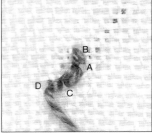

4. Take the thread to the back at C and emerge at D.

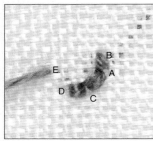

5. Take the thread to the back at C and emerge at E.

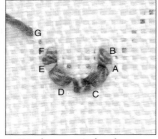

6. Work two stitches between E and D and F and E in the same manner. Emerge at G.

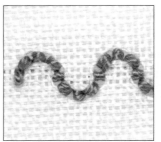

7. Continue working double back stitches to form the wave pattern to the end of the row.

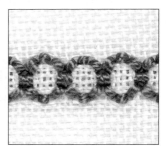

8. Work a mirror image of the previous row, There should be four stitches at each intersection.

ROCOCO (QUEEN) STITCH

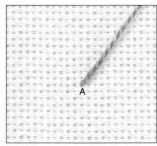

1. Bring the thread to the front at A.

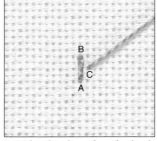

2. Take the thread to the back at B and emerge at C.

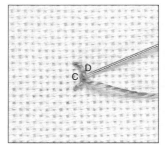

3. Slide the needle from right to left under the stitch. Take the needle to the back at D, one thread to the right of C.

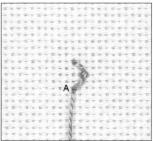

4. Pull the thread through. Emerge at A, through the same hole in the fabric.

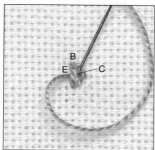

5. Take the thread to the back at B. Emerge at E, two threads below B and insert the needle at C.

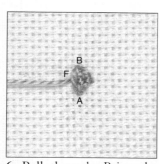

6. Pull through. Bring the thread to the front at A. Take it to the back at B. Emerge at F, two threads below and one to the left of B.

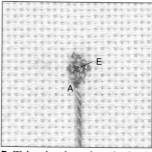

7. Take the thread to the back at E. Emerge at A and pull the thread through.

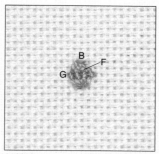

8. Take the thread to the back at B. Emerge at G. Take the needle to the back at F. Pull the thread through.

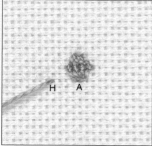

9. Bring the thread to the front at H, four threads to the left of A.

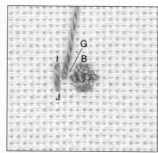

10. Take the thread to the back at I, four threads to the left of B. Emerge at J, one thread to the left of G.

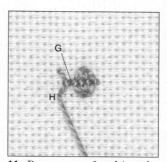

11. Repeat step 3, taking the needle to the back at G. Emerge at H. Pull the thread through.

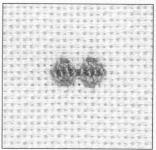

12. Repeat steps 5 to 8 to complete the second stitch.

ROLLED RIBBON ROSE

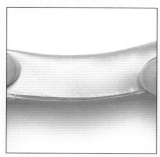

1. Cut a strip of fabric on the bias or use bias cut ribbon. Fold the ribbon in half along the length.

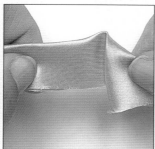

2. With the folded edge at the top, fold down one end diagonally so that a tail of approx 1.5cm (⁵⁄₈") extends below the raw edge.

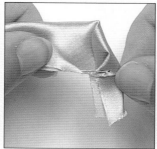

3. Keeping the raw edges even, fold over the end. Take 2 or 3 tiny stitches through the base to secure.

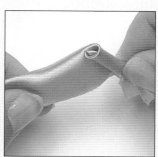

4. Leave the thread hanging free. Still keeping the raw edges even, begin to roll the folded end.

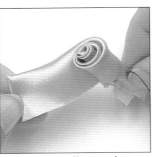

5. Secure the roll with 2 or 3 tiny stitches through all layers at the base.

6. Continue rolling and securing until the rose is the desired size. Cut off excess, leaving a tail the width of the folded ribbon plus 1.5cm (⅝") long.

7. Diagonally fold the ribbon back and down so a 1.5cm (⅝") tail extends below the lower edge.

8. Roll the diagonal end onto the rose. Tightly wrap the thread around the base 3 or 4 times and secure. Trim the tails close to the base.

ROPE STITCH

Different looks can be achieved with rope stitch by varying the width. Place the needle diagonally when working a wide rope stitch and vertically when working a narrow rope stitch.

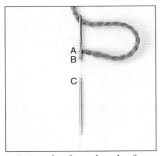

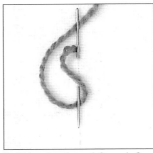

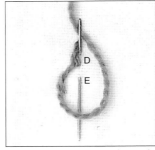

1. Bring the thread to the front at the top of the line at A. Take the needle from B to C.

2. Take the thread from left to right over the needle and then pass it from right to left under the tip of the needle.

3. Pull the thread through. Take the needle from D to E.

4. Take the thread from right to left under the tip of the needle.

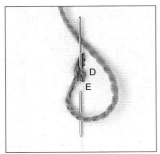

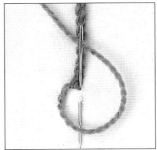

5. Pull thread through. Take the needle to the back just below D and emerge just below E.

6. Continue working stitches in the same manner for the required distance.

7. To finish, take needle to the back of the fabric just below the loop of the last stitch.

8. Pull the thread through and secure on the back of the fabric.

ROSE LEAF STITCH

This unusual stitch can be used to create shaded leaves and buds.
Double a piece of card so that it measures the required size of the loops.

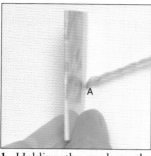

1. Holding the card on the fabric, bring the lightest thread to the surface at A.

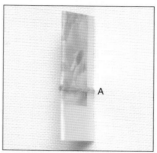

2. Take the thread to the back, over the card and as close to A as possible.

3. Work two more stitches in the same manner. Secure the thread.

4. Change to the medium shade of thread and work three more stitches in the same manner. Secure the thread.

5. Change to the darkest thread and work three more stitches.

6. Slide the card out.

7. Carefully turn the loops inside out, pushing the dark stitches through the light.

8. Bring the thread to the front at the tip of the leaf. Take the needle through the last loop of the darkest thread.

9. Take the thread to the back through the same hole.

10. Work a stem stitch along the centre of the leaf to form a vein.

ROSETTE CHAIN STITCH

This variation of twisted chain produces an attractive, braided line. It is a useful outline stitch and equally effective in straight lines or curves.

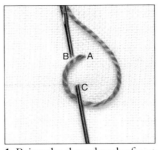

1. Bring the thread to the front at A. Keeping the thread under the needle, insert the needle at B and emerge at C.

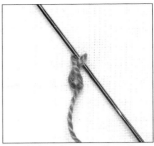

2. Slide the needle, from bottom to top, under the stitch as shown.

3. Pull the thread through, holding the loop in place with your thumb.

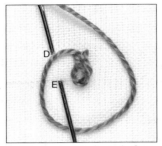

4. Work a second stitch from D to E, keeping the thread under the tip of the needle.

5. Holding the second loop in place, slide the needle under the thread between the stitches.

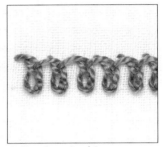

6. Continue in this manner to the end of the row, anchoring the last stitch over the last loop.

ROSETTE STITCH ROSE

These roses are a quick and effective way to add variety to floral embroidery. The needle is inserted into the fabric to form the framework around which the thread is wound. After winding, the thread is couched in place.

1. Bring the needle to the front at A. Insert needle at B, 2-3mm (¹/₈") above A. Emerge at C. Leave the needle in the fabric.

2. Pick up the thread at A. Wrap the thread under each end of the needle in a counter clockwise direction.

3. Work 2 - 3 more wraps in the same manner. Ensure the wraps lie side-by-side and not on top of each other.

4. Holding the wraps in place with your left thumb near the top, gently pull the needle through.

5. Still holding the wraps with your thumb, take the thread over the wraps and to the back of the fabric.

6. Pull the thread through. Bring the needle to the front at the top, inside the last wrap.

7. Take the needle to the back over the last wrap and pull the thread through.

ROUMANIAN STITCH

Also known as Roman stitch, Roumanian stitch can be used as a filling to create a broad outline.

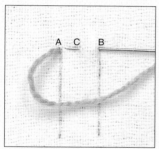 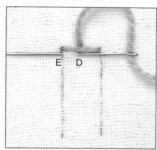 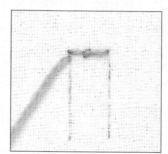 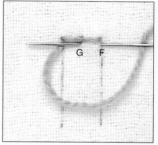

1. Draw two lines on the fabric. Bring the thread to the front at A. Take the needle from B to C. Ensure the thread is below the needle.

2. Pull the thread through. With the thread above the needle, take the needle from D to E.

3. Pull the thread through.

4. Take the needle from F to G. Ensure the thread is below the needle.

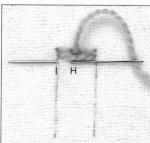 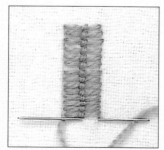  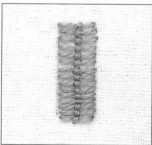

5. Pull the thread through. With the thread above the needle, take the needle from H to I.

6. Pull the thread through. Continue working stitches in the same manner.

7. To finish, work the first half of the last stitch. Take the needle to the back below the straight stitch but do not re-emerge on the left hand side.

8. Pull the thread through and secure on the back of the fabric.

RUNNING STITCH — INTERLACED

This stitch can be worked in a single colour, or two or three colours to create a pretty effect.

Use a tapestry needle and a firm round thread such as cotton perlé when working the interlacing.

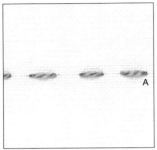

1. Bring the thread to the front at A. Work a line of small running stitches.

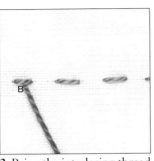

2. Bring the interlacing thread to the surface at B, half way along the last running stitch.

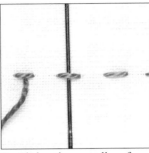

3. Slide the needle, from bottom to top, under the second running stitch.

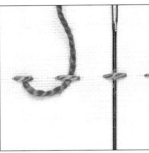

4. Pull thread through. Slide the needle, from top to bottom, under the third running stitch.

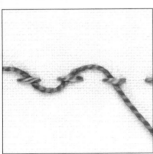

5. Pull thread through. Continue working in this manner, alternating the direction of the interlacing, to the end of the line.

6. Take the thread to the back half way along the first running stitch and secure.

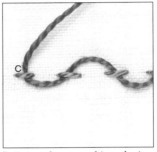

7. Bring the second interlacing thread to the surface at C, half way along the running stitch.

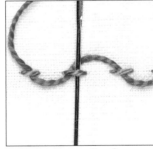

8. Slide the needle, from top to bottom, under the second stitch.

9. Pull thread through. Slide the needle, from bottom to top, under the third stitch.

10. Pull thread through.

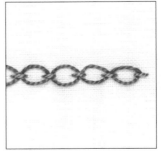

11. Continue working in this manner to the end of the line. Take the thread to the back half way along the running stitch and secure.

SATIN STITCH OUTLINE

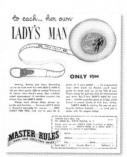

Used in French whitework where it is known as CORDONNET, *this stitch is similar to trailing, but is usually consistent in height and width, so there are no threads added or subtracted. It is worked along a single design line. When worked over a thicker line it is known as* POINT DE BOURDON *or* BOURDON STITCH.

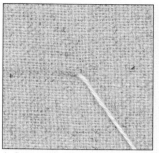

1. Secure the thread. Bring the thread to the front at the beginning of the line.

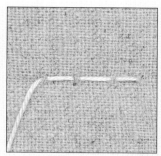

2. Work running stitches along the design line taking only 1 - 2 threads of fabric when making a stitch.

3. Continue working in this manner to the end of the line. You should have long stitches on the top of the fabric and tiny stitches on the back.

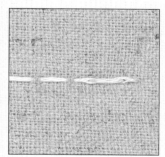

4. Bring the thread to the front at the centre of the first stitch. Take the thread to the back before the centre of the second stitch, splitting the stitch.

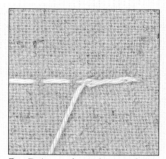

5. Bring thread to front beyond centre of the second stitch, again splitting the stitch. Pick up only 1 - 2 threads of fabric with this stitch.

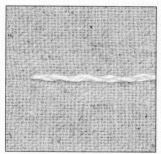

6. Repeat steps 4 and 5, working in this manner to the end of the line.

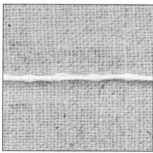

7. Cut a thread 5cm (2") longer than the line. Ensure this 'guide' rests on top of the padding, without being attached, when working the satin stitch.

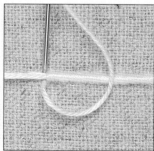

8. Beginning with a new thread, work satin stitches over the padding and guide, angling the needle to maintain a fine line.

SATIN STITCH PADDING

Several layers of satin stitch can be worked to create a dome shape. Horizontal and vertical satin stitches build the surface that the final layer of stitches is worked over.

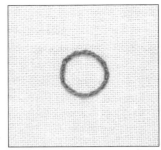

1. Work split stitch around the spot outline.

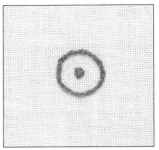

2. Work a small circle of horizontal satin stitches in the centre of the circle.

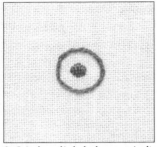

3. Stitch a slightly larger circle of vertical satin stitches over the previous circle.

4. Continue working the circles, alternating between vertical and horizontal stitches.

5. Work the final layer, covering the split stitch outline.

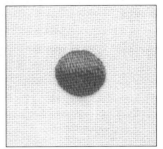

6. Completed satin stitch padding.

SIENNESE STITCH

This stitch is ideal for wide borders and creates a textured line. Mark temporary parallel lines onto the fabric.

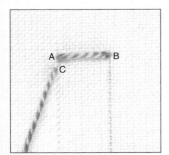

1. Bring the thread to the front at A. Take the thread to the back at B and emerge at C.

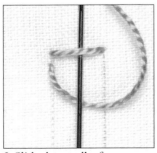

2. Slide the needle, from top to bottom, under the straight stitch, ensuring that the working thread is under the tip of the needle.

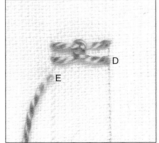

3. Pull thread through. Take the needle to the back at D and emerge at E.

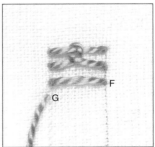

4. Take the thread to the back at F and emerge at G.

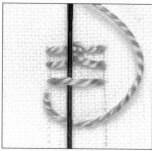

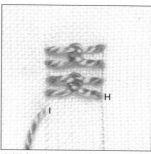

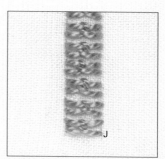

5. Slide the needle, from top to bottom, under the straight stitch, ensuring that the working thread is under the tip of the needle.

6. Take the thread to the back at H and emerge at I.

7. Continue working in this manner to the end of the lines.

8. Take the thread to the back at J and secure.

SINGLE LOOP STITCH

Single loop stitch is similar to Ghiordes knot with each loop worked and secured individually.

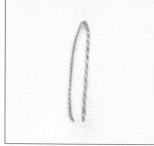

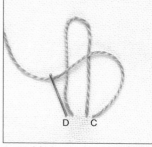

1. Bring the thread to the front at A. Take the needle to the back at B.

2. Pull the thread through, leaving a loop on the front.

3. Hold the loop and emerge at C. Take the needle to the back at D, over the base of the loop.

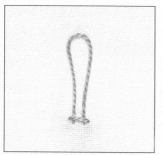

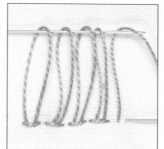

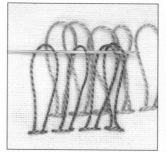

4. Pull the thread through to secure the loop.

5. Continue to work loops along the row in this manner, using a tapestry needle to shape and position the loops.

6. Work a second row of loops below the first in the same manner. Offset the stitches to avoid creating vertical rows.

SORBELLO STITCH

Beautiful as a decorative border, Sorbello stitch can also be used as an isolated motif. Take care not to pull the stitch too tightly. Mark temporary parallel lines onto the fabric.

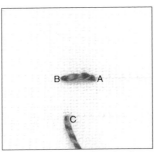

1. Bring the thread to the front at A. Take the thread to the back at B and emerge at C.

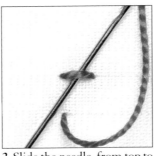

2. Slide the needle, from top to bottom, under the straight stitch. Keep the working thread to the right.

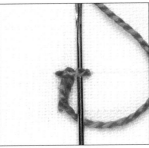

3. Slide the needle, from top to bottom, under the straight stitch. Ensuring that the thread is under the tip of the needle, pull through.

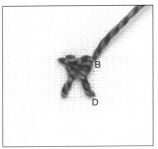

4. Take the needle to the back at D and emerge at B.

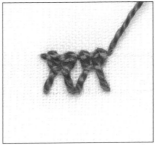

5. Work a second stitch in the same manner.

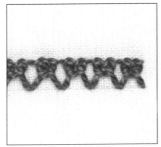

6. Continue working stitches to the end of the line.

STEP FILLING STITCH

Step filling creates a checked surface on even weave fabric. The stitches should not be pulled tightly as in other pulled thread techniques.

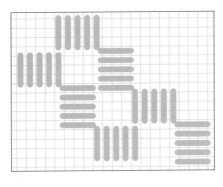

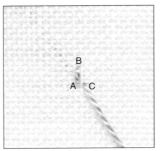

1. Bring the thread to the front at A. Take the thread to the back at B and emerge at C.

2. Work four more vertical straight stitches.

step filling stitch | *continued*

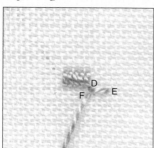

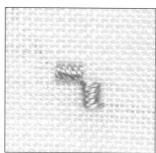

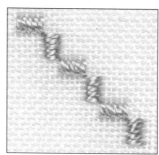

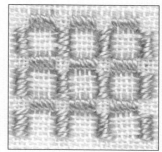

3. Bring the thread to the front at D. Take the thread to the back at E and emerge at F.

4. Work four more horizontal straight stitches.

5. Continue working blocks of five horizontal and five vertical stitches.

6. Work further diagonal rows of vertical and horizontal stitches to fill the shape.

THORN STITCH

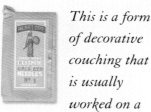

This is a form of decorative couching that is usually worked on a curve but can be worked as a straight line. It is most effective when worked with contrasting threads.

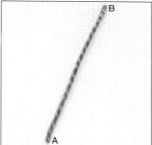

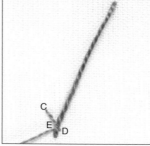

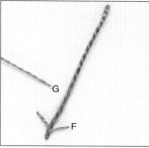

1. Bring the thread to be couched up at A. Take the thread to the back at B and secure.

2. Bring the couching thread to the front at C. Take the thread to the back at D and emerge at E.

3. Take the thread to the back at F and emerge at G.

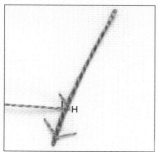

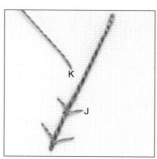

4. Take the thread to the back at H and emerge at I.

5. Take the thread to the back at J and emerge at K.

6. Continue working in this manner to the end of the couching thread.

7. Take the thread to the back at L and secure.

THREE SIDED STITCH

This stitch is also known as point turc (Turkish stitch) and lace stitch. Although primarily a stitch for use on even weave fabrics, it can also be used on finely woven fabrics. Pull each stitch as firmly as possible to open the fabric threads. Use a large needle when working on finely woven fabrics to open large holes in the surface.

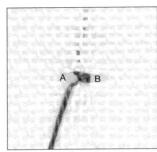

1. Bring the thread to the front at A. Take the thread to the back at B and re-emerge at A.

2. Take the thread to the back at B and re-emerge at A.

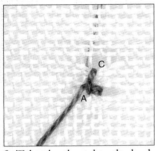

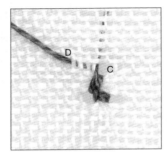

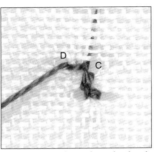

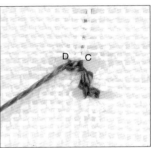

3. Take the thread to the back at C and re-emerge at A.

4. Take the thread to the back at C and emerge at D.

5. Take the thread to the back at C and re-emerge at D.

6. Take the thread to the back at C and re-emerge at D.

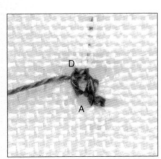

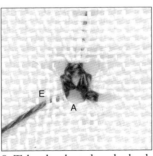

7. Take the thread to the back at A and re-emerge at D.

8. Take the thread to the back at A and emerge at E.

9. Continue working in this manner across the row

Point Turc is particularly beautiful when worked on good quality voile with fine machine sewing thread. This creates a very delicate line of stitched holes that look attractive with fine laces and pintucks.

TRAILING

Trailing is an alternate method of padding that does not involve any preliminary stitching, as the padding threads are simply laid along the design lines. The width of the line is varied by adding or subtracting padding threads.

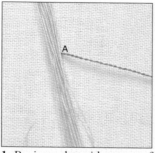

1. Begin at the widest part of the design. Lay the padding threads along design line. Bring thread to front at A.

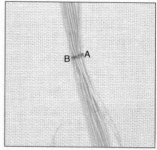

2. Take the thread over the padding threads and to the back at B, on the marked line.

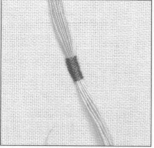

3. Continue working satin stitch over the padding.

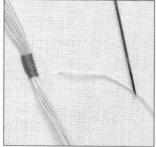

4. Thread one strand of padding. Take to the back within the design lines. Emerge a short distance away.

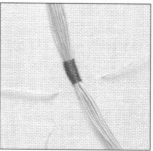

5. Repeat on the other side of the design with a second thread.

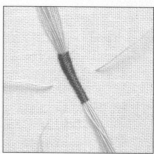

6. Continue working satin stitches over the padding.

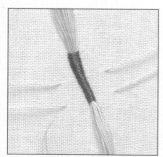

7. Sink two more threads using the same method as steps 4 and 5.

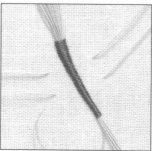

8. Continue working satin stitches over the padding.

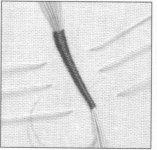

9. Sink two more threads in the same manner as before.

10. Continue working satin stitches along the design line.

133

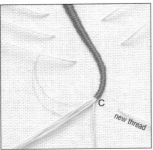

11. To add threads, leave the end of a new padding thread on the front, take it to the back and emerge at C.

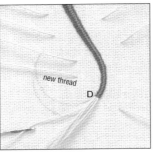

12. Introduce a second new thread on the other side of the padding threads at D.

13. Continue working satin stitches over the padding.

14. Introduce another two threads in the same manner as steps 11 and 12.

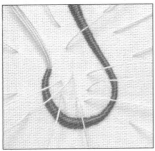

15. Continue working the trailing, increasing and decreasing threads according to the design.

16. Take the remaining threads to the back, two strands at a time.

17. Turn the work over. Pull each padding thread to the back and trim close to the fabric.

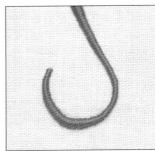

18. Completed trailing.

UNDERSIDE COUCHING

Underside couching is an ancient stitch that was traditionally used for couching precious metal thread onto fabric. It is an excellent way to quickly cover a large background area with thread.

The couching thread should be finer than the couched thread and should be invisible when the work is finished. It is also known as invisible stitch.

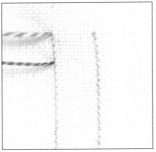

1. Secure the couching thread on the back of the work. Secure the thread to be couched at the top of the line.

2. Take the couching thread over the thicker thread then to the back through the same hole.

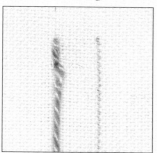 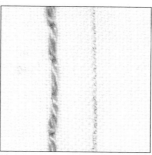  

3. Give the couching thread a slight tug so that a little of the couched thread is pulled to the back.

4. Continue working in this manner, spacing the stitches evenly.

5. Work a second row, off-setting the couching thread to form a brick pattern.

6. Work the number of rows required to fill the shape.

VANDYKE STITCH

Vandyke stitch is an attractive filling stitch that is often used for leaf shapes. It can also be worked as a border.

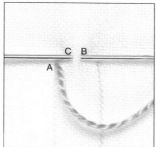 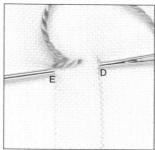 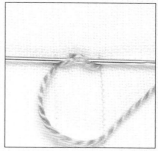

1. Bring the thread to the front at A and make a small stitch from B to C.

2. Pull the thread firmly and take a stitch from D to E.

3. Slide the needle, from right to left, under the crossed threads without piercing the fabric.

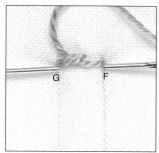  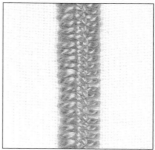 

4. Pull the thread firmly, insert the needle at F and emerge at G.

5. Slide the needle, from right to left, under the crossed threads.

6. Continue working in this manner to the end of the shape.

WAVE FILLING STITCH

Also known as straight line stitch, wave filling creates quite a dense but lacy overall pattern.

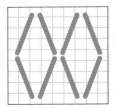

Pull each stitch as firmly as possible to open the fabric threads.

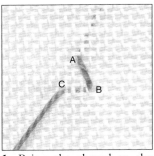

1. Bring the thread to the surface at A. Take the thread to the back at B and emerge at C.

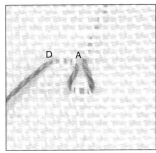

2. Take the thread to the back at A and emerge at D.

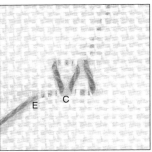

3. Take the thread to the back at C and emerge at E.

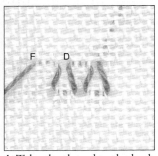

4. Take the thread to the back at D and emerge at F.

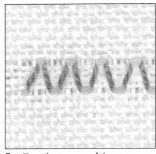

5. Continue working across the row in this manner.

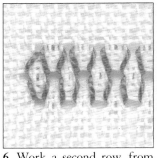

6. Work a second row, from left to right, mirror imaging the first row to form diamonds.

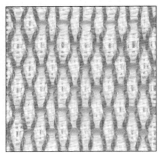

7. Continue working rows until the shape is full.

WHIPPED RUNNING STITCH

Whipped running stitch is worked in two stages and has a raised corded appearance. It is particularly effective when worked with two thread colours. Use a tapestry needle to work the whipping stitches. Mark a line onto the fabric.

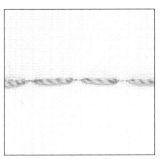

1. Work a line of running stitches, keeping the space between each stitch small.

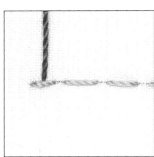

2. Bring the second thread to the front above the centre of the first running stitch.

 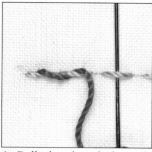  

3. Slide the needle, from bottom to top, under the second stitch.

4. Pull the thread through. Slide the needle, from bottom to top, under the third stitch.

5. Continue working in this manner to the end of the row

6. To end off, take the needle to the back under the centre of the last running stitch and secure.

WHIPPED DOUBLE RUNNING STITCH

By adding a second row of whipping, a third colour can be introduced and the corded effect is emphasised. Alternatively, work all three thread passes in the same colour. Use a tapestry needle to work the whipping stitch. Mark a line onto the fabric.

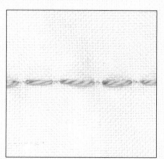  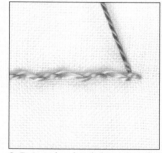 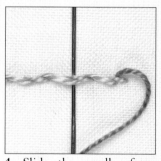

1. Work a line of running stitches along the marked line.

2. Whip the running stitch following the instructions for *Whipped running stitch.*

3. Bring the third thread to the front above the centre of the first stitch.

4. Slide the needle, from bottom to top, under the second stitch.

  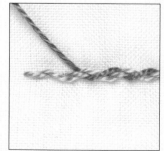 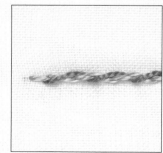

5. Pull the thread through loosely.

6. Slide the needle, from bottom to top, under the third running stitch.

7. Pull the thread through loosely. Continue in this manner to the end of the row.

8. Take the needle to the back over the centre of the last running stitch and secure.

WHIPPED SPLIT STITCH

Split stitch is an excellent line and filling stitch. By whipping the stitches extra colour and interest can be added very easily. When whipping the stitch, use a tapestry needle.

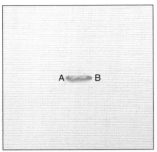

1. Bring the needle to the front at A. Take the needle to the back at B. Pull the thread through.

2. Emerge in the middle of the stitch, splitting the thread with the needle.

3. Pull the thread through. Take the needle to the back at C.

4. Pull the thread through. Emerge through the middle of the second stitch, splitting the thread.

5. Pull the thread through. Continue working stitches in the same manner to the end of the line.

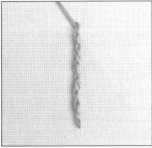

6. Bring the needle to the front, under middle of first split stitch.

7. Slide the needle from right to left under the upper half of the second split stitch.

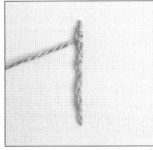

8. Pull the thread through until the stitch rests against the split stitch.

9. Slide the needle from right to left under the upper half of the third split stitch.

10. Pull thread through. Continue in this manner to the end of the line.

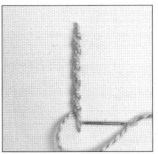

11. Take the needle to the back under the last split stitch.

12. Completed whipped split stitch.

WINDOW FILLING STITCH

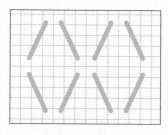

Window filling is a more open variation of wave filling and also creates a lacy pattern. Pull each stitch firmly to open the fabric threads.

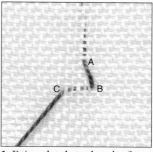

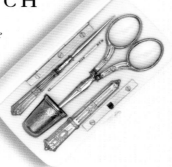

1. Bring the thread to the front at A. Take the thread to the back at B and emerge at C.

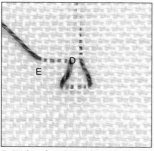

2. Take the thread to the back at D and emerge at E.

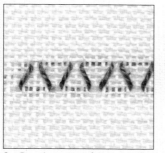

3. Continue working in this manner to the end of the row.

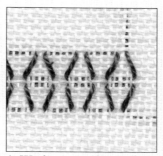

4. Work a second row, from left to right, as a mirror image of the first leaving one free thread between the rows.

5. Continue working rows until the shape is full.

WOVEN BAND — DIAGONAL

Diagonal woven band creates a heavy line that is diagonally striped. It can be worked with most types of thread. Mark parallel lines onto the fabric.

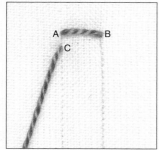

1. Bring the thread to the front at A. Take the thread to the back at B and emerge at C.

2. Continue working evenly spaced horizontal stitches for the required distance.

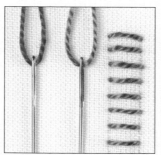

3. Thread two needles, one with each stripe colour.

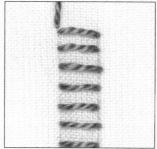

4. Bring colour 1 to the front above the left end of the first bar.

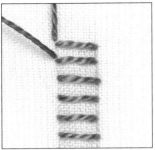 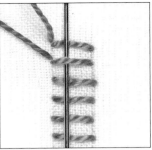 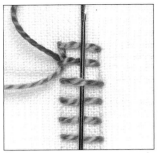 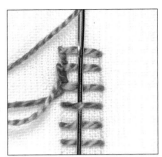

5. Bring colour 2 to the front above the left end of the second bar and lie the thread to the left.

6. Slide the needle with colour 1 from top to bottom under the second bar.

7. Lie the thread to the left. Bring colour 2 over colour 1 and slide the needle from top to bottom under the third bar.

8. Lie the thread to the left. Bring colour 1 over colour 2 and slide the needle from top to bottom under the fourth bar.

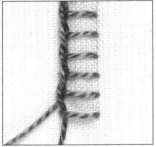   

9. Continue working in this manner to the end of the line.

10. Secure the two threads over the last bar.

11. Bring colour 2 to the front above the first bar. Bring colour 1 to the front above the second bar.

12. Work a second line of alternating stitches in the same manner as the first.

13. Fill the woven bars with row of stitches, alternating the colours to form diagonal stripes.

Working woven bands

Cutting the weaving threads long enough to cover the foundation bars, will ensure there are no joins, keeping a continuous flow to the band.

Packing the rows of weaving threads firmly around the foundation bars will help create a smooth neat surface, with no foundation bars visible.

WOVEN BAND — STRIPED

This is worked in the same manner as diagonal woven band but each row begins with the same colour so that horizontal stripes are formed. Mark parallel lines onto the fabric.

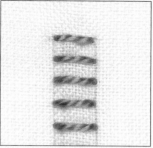

1. Work a series of evenly spaced horizontal bars between the two marked lines.

2. Bring colour 1 to the front above the left end of the first bar.

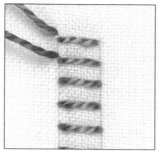

3. Bring colour 2 to the front above the left end of the second bar and lie the thread to the left.

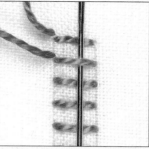

4. Slide the needle with colour 1 under the second bar.

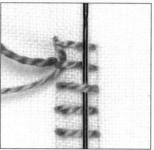

5. Lie the thread to the left. Slide the needle with colour 2 under the third bar.

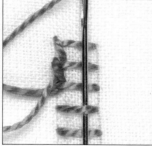

6. Lie the thread to the left. Bring colour 1 over colour 2 and slide the needle under the fourth bar.

7. Continue alternating colours to the end of the row. Secure the two threads over the last bar.

8. Continue working rows in this manner until the shape is filled.

INDEX

BIBLIOGRAPHY

A - Z of Embroidery Stitches
Country Bumpkin Publications 1997

Erica Wilson's Embroidery Book
Charles Scribner's Sons New York 1973

Marion Nichols Encyclopedia of Embroidery Stitches including Crewel
Dover New York 1974

Mary Thomas's Dictionary of Embroidery Stitches
New Edition by Jan Eaton
Hodder and Stoughton London 1991

The Coats Book of Embroidery by Mary Gostelow
Paul Hamlyn Pty Ltd 1978